The Social Economy of West Germany

Graham Hallett, M.A., Ph.D.

Senior Lecturer in Economics
University College, Cardiff

MACMILLAN

First published 1973 by
THE MACMILLAN PRESS LTD
London and Basingstoke
Associated companies in New York
Dublin Melbourne Johannesburg and Madras

SBN 333 14877 0

Printed in Great Britain by
R. AND R. CLARK LTD
Edinburgh

To Veronica

Contents

Act: Recovery and Inflation: External Problems:
Professor Schiller's Resignation

Preface

Why should we study the 'social economy' of West Germany? One practical reason why Germany (and France) are often selected for 'European studies' courses in the United Kingdom is that most British students obtain some acquaintance with the language of one or other country. But there are more profound reasons. The German Federal Republic is economically the most important member of the European Community which Britain has just joined, and is rapidly gaining political power to match its economic power. An understanding of its economic and social structure is therefore of considerable topical importance. At a more academic level, the United Kingdom and the German Federal Republic provide interesting opportunities for comparative studies. Many political and social movements which originated in Germany have influenced Great Britain – e.g. Bismarckian socialism. The reverse has also happened: this was especially marked in the early nineteenth century, when British liberal thinkers had considerable influence in Germany, but there have been more recent examples. British administrators, ironically enough, were mainly responsible for achieving the reform in trade unions in West Germany which they failed to achieve in their own country. Because of the comparable status of Great Britain and Germany, and their cultural affinities, they provide an interesting comparison. Although it is never possible to isolate completely the effect of differing policies, some indications can be obtained from countries which have a good deal in common but have adopted differing policies.

West Germany and the United Kingdom are both medium-sized European states with similar problems: an uncomfortable Eastern neighbour, a diminishing American military umbrella, the growing concern with environmental pollution and the 'quality of life'. Both have had problems in finding their level in the world, although in different ways. Britain ended the War thinking of itself as one of the 'big four', and as possessing a world status which its population or economic power no longer justified. Its postwar history has therefore been largely one of an adjustment – voluntary or forced – to a more modest role. The complacency arising from having 'won' the war also inhibited reforms of the structure of industry and labour relations in Britain, leading to a decline in competitive ability. West Germany by contrast had suffered a traumatic military defeat, her economic system had been destroyed, and her cities were in ruins. Her rapid subsequent recovery, although in no way 'miraculous', has had few parallels in history (one of them being also in German history – the recovery in the seventeenth century from the devastation of the Thirty Years War to the glory of the baroque era).

On the whole however West Germany has not had a good press in the United Kingdom. In so far as most British intellectuals have seen anything good in continental Western Europe outside Scandinavia, it has been in France rather than Germany. Mr Andrew Shonfield, for example, in his influential book *Modern Capitalism*[1] maintained that West Germany and the United States were 'not in the mainstream of modern capitalism', which was represented by France; the French system of 'indicative planning' was held up as a model for Britain, and strongly influenced the 'National Plan 1965–1970'. Less has been heard of French planning since the riots of May 1968 and their aftermath, and subsequent studies have questioned some of the conclusions reached by Mr Shonfield (who nevertheless, as always, put his finger on a number of important points).[2]

Much of the discussion of the economies of the United Kingdom and West Germany has concentrated on 'economic planning' in the sense of central control of the economy.[3] I have tried to encompass a wider field. Formal 'planning' by the central government is only one – and often not the most important – of the factors governing the performance (in the widest sense) of an economy, and one whose importance has

[1] Oxford University Press, for the Royal Institute of International Affairs, 1965.

[2] V. Lutz, *Central Planning for the Economy; An Analysis of the French Theory and Experience* (Longmans, 1969).

[3] G. Denton and others, *Economic Planning and Policies in Britain, France and Germany* (Allen & Unwin, 1968).

perhaps been overemphasised in Britain in the 1960s. The driving force in any economy comes from below – from the skills, attitudes and character of its people, and from the working arrangements in factories, farms, offices, universities. Misguided government policies can frustrate the natural energies of a people, but 'planning' can do little to compensate for structural weaknesses; a racehorse can be turned into a carthorse by putting it between the shafts and in blinkers, but a carthorse cannot be turned into a racehorse by putting it in racing colours. The German 'economic miracle' was achieved under a system explicitly designed to 'set the people free', which had been violently attacked by advocates of a more planned economy, who had forecast economic and social disaster. Faced with German achievements, the advocates of 'indicative planning' in the 1960s were in something of a dilemma. Some denied German achievements, some suggested that West Germany was in fact a more planned economy than it seemed, although few went so far as Professor Oulès, who compared Dr Ludwig Erhard with Goebbels.[1]

This book attempts to describe and assess some of the main characteristics of the economic and the social structure of West Germany – hence the title 'social economy'. This is a somewhat broader canvas than economics, as generally understood. Academic economists have tended to apply sophisticated techniques to an extremely limited field, and to ignore the institutional, social and political factors which are of so much importance in economic life. This has led to a widespread disillusionment with economics among practical men. If economists are to contribute to the understanding of public affairs, they will have to pay more attention to economic and social institutions, as did many of the great economists of the past – for example, Adam Smith, J. S. Mill and Alfred Marshall. From that point of view, this little book can perhaps be regarded as a straw in the wind.

I have had occasion to study the German Federal Republic for many years and – in spite of some apprehensions about the future – I have seen far more to like than to dislike. In dealing with some contentious issues I make no claim to be impartial,

[1] Firmin Oulès, *Economic Planning and Democracy* (Penguin Books, 1966) p. 327.

but I have tried to be fair and to make my value judgements explicit; economists and sociologists who claim to be 'value-free' generally smuggle their value judgements in through the back door. The limitations of space have enforced some selectivity, but I have tried to deal with those aspects which seem at present the most important.

May 1973 GRAHAM HALLETT

Acknowledgements

The author would like to thank all those people in West Germany who were so generous with their assistance when he was preparing material – the staff of the Library of the *Institut für Weltwirtschaft* in Kiel, former colleagues in agricultural economics, civil servants, and spokesmen for industry and trade unions. He is indebted to the Alexander von Humboldt Foundation both for the Research Fellowship which originally brought him to Germany and for a Travel Scholarship in connection with this book.

1 Basic Facts and Figures

Land and Population

Some quantitative comparisons of West Germany with the United Kingdom may help to put the subsequent discussion of the West German economy into perspective. West Germany and the United Kingdom are very similar in land area and population (table 1), and their overall population densities of over 200 persons per square kilometre are among the highest in the world. However the geographical distribution of the population differs considerably. In the United Kingdom there

Table 1

PEOPLE AND LAND 1970

	Area (000 sq. km.)	Population 1970 (million)	Population (per sq. km.)	Estimated Population 1980 (million)
West Germany	249	61·5	248	63·5
United Kingdom	244	55·7	228	58·9

Source: All tables in this chapter, unless otherwise stated, are taken from *Basic Statistics of the Community*, 1972, published by the E.E.C. Commission.

Table 2

DISTRIBUTION OF LABOUR FORCE BY INDUSTRIES 1970 (thousand)

	Agriculture	Manufacturing	Services	Unemployed	Total
West Germany	2406	13,247	11,052	149	26,854
United Kingdom	715	11,714	12,475	555	25,459

is a strong concentration of population in the capital, with no other urban centre of comparable standing. West Germany on the other hand has some six conurbations, all of comparable size, as well as a larger proportion of its population in medium-sized towns of under 500,000.[1]

[1] For a survey of the problems of London, Paris and the Rhein—Ruhr complex see Peter Hall, *The World Cities* (Weidenfeld & Nicolson, 1966).

In the vocational distribution of the labour force the most striking difference is in the numbers engaged in agriculture – 14% in West Germany as compared with 3·5% in the United Kingdom. The main reason for the difference is that Germany did not experience the British enclosure movement at the eighteenth and early nineteenth centuries. From the end of the nineteenth century onwards the emphasis of German policy was on protection rather than structural adaptation. Since 1945, in spite of continued protection, the West German countryside has been opened up to the pressures of an industrial economy; the effect has been to drag it rather violently into the twentieth century.

National Income

In 1958 the United Kingdom had a higher national income (in total and *per capita*) than West Germany. In 1970 *per capita* income in Germany was nearly 50% higher than in the United Kingdom. These figures – like all international comparisons of national income – need to be treated with caution. They are based on current exchange rates, and do not take account of differences in price level between the two countries. To arrive at an indicator of real income, the figures should be deflated by a price index. This international comparison of price levels is problematical; it is difficult to obtain representative quotations and different figures will be obtained according to the consumption pattern used for weighting. Comparisons of the cost of living published in the German *Statistical Yearbook* suggest that, over most of the 1960s, the German price level was comparable with that in the United Kingdom, but rose above it after 1967; in 1971 it was 10–20% higher.[1] Thus the national-income figures probably exaggerate the difference in living standards, but still suggest that the 'standard of living' is higher in West Germany than in Britain. Differences in the *rate of growth* of national income (deflated for price changes) are easier to measure, and there is no doubt that the West German figure

---

[1] *Statistisches Jahrbuch 1972.* Internationale Übersichten, p. 110. The calculation is expressed – rather confusingly – in terms of the purchasing power of the Deutschmark, and two rates are calculated. Up to 1967, the official rate (in D.M. per £) was between the two purchasing power rates. After that it was below both, by roughly 10% and 20% respectively.

has been higher than the British, even in the 1960s, when recovery from the war had been completed. At the same time the average number of hours worked in German industry has dropped, and is now below the British figure.

Table 3
GROSS NATIONAL PRODUCT AT CURRENT PRICES
($ million)

	1958 Total	1970 Total	1970 Per capita ($)
Germany (F.R.)	59,200	186,000	3031
United Kingdom	64,800	121,400	2179

Table 4
AVERAGE ANNUAL GROWTH RATES OF G.N.P. AT
CONSTANT PRICES 1960–70

	Total %	Per capita %	Per person employed %
Germany (F.R.)	4·8	3·7	4·4
United Kingdom	2·8	2·2	2·6

Table 5
HOURS AND WAGES: WAGE EARNERS IN MANUFAC-
TURING INDUSTRY, 1970.

	Average weekly hours	Average hourly earnings (new pence)
Germany (F.R.)	39·1	78p
United Kingdom	44·9	65p

A useful check on national income figures is provided by physical measures of consumption. Some figures for food and other items are given in tables 6(a) and 6(b); these at least suggest that some of the stories put out during the Common Market debate, to the effect that the continentals could not afford meat or medical attention, were wide of the mark.

It is, of course, absurd to make a fetish of material living standards or economic growth. But whether economic growth is good or bad depends on the use to which it is put. It can

Table 6 (a)

FOOD CONSUMPTION 1970 (KG. PER HEAD PER YEAR)

	Cereals	Potatoes	Vegetables	Wine (litres)	Meat	Butter	Milk
Germany (F.R.)	66	102	65	16	74	7·2	78
United Kingdom	73	98	62	3	73	7·0	143

Table 6(b)

OTHER INDICATORS OF LIVING STANDARDS 1970

	Crude steel consumption (kg. per head)	Passenger cars (million)	Telephones (per 1000 pop.)	Doctors (per 100,000 pop.)	Hosp. beds
Germany (F.R.)	659	13·9	212	154	1102
United Kingdom	438	11·8	153	113	972

produce 'public affluence and public squalor' (to quote Professor Galbraith's description of the United States in the 1950s) but it can also be used to create a more civilised environment. In West Germany, where vast sums have been spent on theatres and sports facilities as well as on motorways or urban renewal, the impression gained by most visitors is that there is one of the highest levels of public affluence of any country in the world (certainly higher than in the United Kingdom or the United States).

Economists have not achieved much success in giving a purely economic explanation of why different economies grow at different rates.[1] It is becoming increasingly apparent that, often allowing for differences in investment, education etc., the crucial factor is the unexplained 'residual', i.e. psychological climate and social institutions.

West Germany differs from the United Kingdom not only in the level of national income, but also in the uses to which it is put. Throughout the postwar era, the United Kingdom has tended to invest less than West Germany (both in public investment such as motorways and in private investment in industrial plant) and to consume more. The figures in table 7, showing a lower level of capital investment equivalent to about 6% of G.N.P., are typical for the 1960s. The lower level of public investment in the United Kingdom was the result of

[1] E. F. Denison and J.-P. Poulier, *Why Growth Rates Differ* (1967).

Table 7

USE OF GROSS DOMESTIC PRODUCT 1970
(per cent)

	Private consumption	Public consumption	Capital investment	Balancing item	Total
Germany (F.R.)	54·2	15·8	26·5	3·5	100
United Kingdom	62·5	18·3	17·8	1·4	100

decisions by governments. The lower level of investment by businesses is more complex. In some cases however poor performance by an industry can cause it to lose markets, thus reducing the scope for new investment. A typical case is the comparative performance of Vauxhall and Opel. Both are subsidiaries of General Motors, and produce basically similar cars. In the 1950s Vauxhall produced many times as many cars as Opel, but as a result of consistently poorer detail design, poorer workmanship, and repeated strikes, the position has been reversed, so that Vauxhall now produces only one quarter the output of Opel, earns much lower profits, and is an unattractive competitor for investment from the parent company.

Inflation

In the postwar era nearly all countries have experienced the problem of a steady, persistent rise in prices. In the 1950s it seemed as though West Germany had discovered the secret of (relative) price stability. In that decade the index of retail prices rose, on average, by around 1·5 % and wholesale prices remained virtually constant. But, in the early 1960s, the curve of the German price level began to slope upwards. This acceleration

Table 8

CHANGE IN RETAIL PRICES 1950–70

	Average annual change %	1970 prices (1950 = 100)
Germany (F.R.)	+ 2·3	160
United Kingdom	+ 4·1	220

Source: Bundesministerium für Wirtschaft und Finanzen, *20 Jahre Leistung in Zahlen 1970*, p. 25.

was dampened by the slight German recession of 1966/7 but gathered strength after 1969, rising to 4–5% between 1970 and 1972 (and to 6–7% in 1973).

The cause of this inflation is as simple as it is difficult to tackle – the monopoly position of trade unions in a period of low unemployment. In Germany, the trade unions exercised restraint in wage claims in the difficult years when the country was still recovering from the war. A further factor encouraging price stability was the memory in Germany of the disastrous hyper-inflation of 1922. But with the passage of time, the readiness to exercise restraint on patriotic grounds has declined and the memories of 1922 have faded.

Table 9
WAGES, OUTPUT AND COSTS

| | Output per man-hour in manufacturing | | Hourly earnings in manufacturing | | Wage costs per unit of output | | Consumer prices | |
	Germany	U.K.	Germany	U.K.	Germany	U.K.	Germany	U.K.
				1963 = 100				
1967	126	118	132	130	105	110	111	115
1968	137	125	138	140	101	112	113	121
1969	144	127	151	151	104	117	115	127
1970	147	131	170	171	115	132	120	135
1971	153	138	190	194	124	142	127	148

Source: *National Institute Economic Review*, May 1972, p. 82.

Taxation

In both countries, the state receives and spends a large proportion of the national income. The proportion taken in taxes is markedly higher in the United Kingdom than in West Germany, but the proportion taken in social security contributions is lower. Since compulsory social security contributions are really a form of tax, it makes sense to add them to taxes. When this is done, total government receipts, as a percentage of G.N.P., are fairly close – 38·6 and 40·4 for Germany and the United Kingdom in 1969. The distribution of tax revenue between indirect taxes (purchase tax, value added tax), taxes on corporations and taxes on individuals is fairly similar in Germany and the United Kingdom, although Germany does not have the very high British rates on large incomes. The highest

Table 10
GOVERNMENT EXPENDITURES AND RECEIPTS 1969
(per cent of G.N.P.)

| | Government Expenditure | | | | | | Receipts | | | |
	Consumption	Investment	Public debt	Current transfers	Capital transfers	Total*	Taxes	Social Security Contributions	Other	Total
Germany (F.R.)	15·8	3·9	1·0	15·5	1·9	37·4	25·2	10·9	2·5	38·6
United Kingdom	17·9	4·8	4·2	10·8	4·6	41·1	31·0	4·9	4·5	40·4

*excluding depreciation

Table 11
BREAKDOWN OF TAX REVENUE 1969

	Total tax revenue (million $)	Indirect taxes	Taxes on corporations (% of total tax revenue)	Taxes on individuals
Germany (F.R.)	38,586	58·1	8·9	33·0
United Kingdom	34,030	55·5	7·8	36·7

marginal rate in 1972 was 56% in Germany as against 85% or
more in the United Kingdom.

Unemployment

In recent years West Germany has experienced the lowest
unemployment rates of any country. The high unemployment
(7–9%) which emerged after the currency reform of 1948 was
taken up as the economy expanded in the early 1950s. Since
the late 1950s, the German economy – except in the short
recession of 1966/7 – has been running at less than 1% unemployment. The number of vacancies has also been higher than
the number of unemployed, which suggests that there has been
virtually no unemployment, except of a transitory nature
(although the German trade unions do not accept this view).

An unusual, but illuminating way of looking at the employment situation (adopted by the National Institute) is to deduct
the number of unemployed from the number of unfilled
vacancies. The results bring out clearly the extremely high
demand for labour in Germany (table 12).

Table 12
'DEMAND FOR LABOUR' (UNFILLED VACANCIES MINUS UNEMPLOYED)
(thousands)

	1965	1966	1967	1968	1969	1970	1971
Germany (F.R.)	+ 502	+ 379	− 158	+ 164	+ 586	+ 646	+ 435
United Kingdom	− 43	− 68	− 338	− 353	− 335	− 389	− 614

Source: *National Institute Economic Review*.

External Trade

West Germany is now the world's second largest trading nation.
With 12·3% of world exports in 1970, it was second only to the
United States as an exporter. The British figure was 6·9%.
These figures include only 'visible' trade (i.e. goods), as distinct
from 'invisible' – commercial services, tourism etc. The United
Kingdom earns a substantial surplus on 'invisible' trade,
whereas Germany has a deficit (the ubiquitous German tourist,
remittances from *Gastarbeiter* etc.). These 'invisible' items,
together with capital flows, largely account for the differences
in table 13 between the value of exports and imports.

Table 13
EXPORTS AND IMPORTS 1970

	Exports as a percentage of G.N.P.	Total exports (\$ thousand million)	Total imports
Germany (F.R.)	18·3	34·2	29·8
United Kingdom	16·2	19·3	21·7

Transport

Although their industrial structures are quite similar, the transport systems of West Germany and the United Kingdom differ in several respects, as a result of both geography and policy. West Germany has retained a larger rail network than the United Kingdom, which carries more passengers, and much more freight. It is a sobering thought that West Germany – in spite of its superior motorway system – uses the railways for 72 milliard (i.e. 000 m.) ton-kilometres of freight against the United Kingdom's 23, and uses inland waterways for 47 milliard ton as against a relatively negligible quantity in the United Kingdom. The *Bundesbahn* is extensively electrified, and unquestionably the most comfortable railway system in the world. These achievements have been at the cost of heavy subsidies; West Germany has, at least implicitly, rejected the 'Beeching' philosophy that railways should be made to pay or be closed. West Germany also makes extensive use of waterways. This is partly the result of possessing navigable rivers; a further reason is that the canals, built later than the British ones, were much wider and thus better suited to modern requirements. The canal network is still being extended. West Germany also has an extensive motorway system; some 2000 kilometres had already been built in the 1930s, but the Federal Republic has also built motorways at twice the British rate.

The Environment

Anyone who travels through West Germany is struck by the extensive, and in many ways attractive, rebuilding of its cities. The situation facing the West German cities at the end of the war was incomparably more catastrophic than in France or the United Kingdom. West Germany had not only lost a fifth of its

Table 14
TRANSPORT 1970

| | Rail | | | Inland waterways | | Road | |
	Length of line operated (km.)	Passenger-kilometres (million)	Ton-kilometres (million)	Length of waterways in use (km.)	Ton-kilometres (million)	Length of motorways (000 km.)	Commercial vehicles in use (000)
Germany (F.R.)	29,694	36,355	71,996	4353	47,175	4·1	1201
United Kingdom	19,470	29,612	23,039	603	140	1·1	1945

housing stock but also faced an influx of millions of refugees. The subsequent building programme was – in its speed and size – without parallel in history. Although the serious housing shortage has since been overcome, housebuilding has continued at a high level to meet the demand for bigger and better accommodation. In the German countryside, the most notable difference from Britain – apart from the different farm and field layout discussed below – is the large wooded area. Nearly a third of the land area of West Germany is covered by forests, well tended and increasingly used for recreation.

Table 15
AGRICULTURAL AND FORESTRY LAND 1969
(000 hectares)

	Wooded area	*Agricultural area*
Germany (F.R.)	7207	13,578
United Kingdom	1750	19,368

Conclusion

These statistical comparisons – and others which could be made – indicate that the German Federal Republic is a country comparable in many ways to the United Kingdom. In economic terms, it has been more successful. With a very similar population, land area and natural resources, it has achieved both a higher material standard of living and also in some ways a more satisfactory physical environment. In terms of social institutions, the West German picture is more mixed. The system of industrial relations is very successful. The system of social security is extensive, but with both good and less good points. In two fields however – Universities and the armed forces – the Federal Republic has failed badly. To explain these social achievements and failures, we must make a more detailed examination, beginning with a brief review of German history.

NOTE: *Statistical Sources*

The comparison of statistics from different countries is fraught with pitfalls. It is best to take statistics from international publications, in which statisticians have done their best to ensure comparability. These include publications of the E.E.C. Commission (*Basic Statistics of the Community*), and of the O.E.C.D. (*Main Economic Indicators*). The *Statistisches Handbuch* published by the German Statistical Office also contains a useful international section, and current developments are well documented in the *Jahresbericht der Bundesregierung*, published by the Presse- und Informationsamt.

2 Historical and Philosophical Background

The economic and social situation in the German Federal Republic cannot be understood without some knowledge of German history.[1] It is only possible here to indicate very briefly some of the main trends which have contributed to the post-1945 situation. The course of Germany's history since the beginning of the nineteenth century has been dominated by its late unification, and the way in which that unification was accomplished. At the beginning of the century, Germany was divided into thirty-nine virtually independent states. This had important economic consequences. Since each state levied tariffs on goods passing its frontiers, the development of trade and industry was hampered, and German manufacturers found it difficult to compete with Great Britain. These circumstances influenced the doctrines of the most eminent German economist of the early nineteenth century, Friedrich List (1789–1846). To encourage the growth of industry, he pleaded for a freeing of trade between the German states, and the building of a national railway system – as well as improved education and political freedom. However he rejected the view of the British 'classical' economists that free trade was always beneficial, arguing that a relatively under-developed country like Germany needed a (modest) protective tariff until it had built up its competitive strength. (A custom's union, with an external tariff, was in fact achieved in 1842, although political unification was unfortunately not brought about by the liberal movements of 1848, but only by the 'blood and iron' regime of Bismarck's Prussia in 1871.) List's economic philosophy is significant; the view

[1] The two best introductory histories – both examples of German prose at its best – are Golo Mann, *Deutsche Geschichte des 19. und 20. Jahrhunderts* (S. Fischer Verlag, 1958) and Gustav Stolper, *Deutsche Wirtschaft seit 1870* (J. C. B. Mohr, 1964). Both are available in translation; *The German Economy 1870 to the Present* (Weidenfeld & Nicolson, 1968) and *The History of Germany since 1789* (Chatto & Windus, 1968).

that the 'invisible hand' of the market was always right, that the government had no role in economic affairs, which sank so deeply into British nineteenth-century thought, was never accepted in Germany. Even liberals, who favoured free trade and the market economy, were ready to accept the need for government intervention when fundamental structural changes were involved.

The German Empire

The unification of Germany in 1872 under Prussian leadership meant the incorporation into the new state of ideals developed in this most Eastern and, in some ways, least German of the German states – integrity, discipline, obedience to authority, an absolutist political system. It was the army and the civil service which had power and status in society, not industrialists. A great deal of economic activity was state-owned or state-controlled, and often run very efficiently.[1]

But although there was much to admire in the Bismarckian Reich – the provisions for social security and public education, an efficient civil service and well-run municipal or state enterprises – there were great dangers when so much state power was uncontrolled by political democracy, and when the Prussian concepts of duty were combined with ideas which had been developing throughout Germany from early in the century – doctrines of racial superiority and anti-Semitism; liberal Western values were rejected and force and conquest glorified.[2] These schools of thought rejected the economic pluralism of the market economy just as much as the political liberalism with which it was associated in Anglo-Saxon countries. And they survived the shock of German defeat in the First World War. Indeed the almost complete state control of economic life during the war showed the possibility of a far more thoroughgoing system of state socialism than the 'handicapped capitalism' (Professor Dahrendorf's phrase) prevailing under the Empire.

[1] 'In Germany an exceptionally large part of the best intellect in the nation seeks for employment under Government, and there is probably no other Government which contains within itself so much trained ability of the highest order. On the other hand, the energy, the originality and the daring which make the best men of business in England and America have but recently been fully developed in Germany; while the German people have a great faculty for obedience.' A. Marshall, *Principles of Economics*, 8th ed. (1920), App. A, p. 753.

[2] Hans Kohn, *The Mind of Germany* (New York, 1960).

In 1916 a Professor of political science at the University of Munster wrote:

> However the war may end, we are the exemplary people. Our ideals will determine the goals of mankind. . . . Impelled by the needs of war, the socialist idea has taken hold of German economic life; its organisation has coalesced in a new spirit, and thus the defence of our nation has given birth to the new idea of 1914, an idea destined for the whole of mankind, the idea of German organisation, the folk-community of national socialism.[1]

Weimar and National Socialism

Under the Weimar Republic many liberalising changes were introduced – in industrial relations and education as well as in political organisation – which have in many cases been taken up by the Federal Republic. But the Weimar Republic started badly, with the hyper-inflation of 1922, which ruined many middle-class holders of financial assets, and it suffered from an insufficiently wide basis of popular support. Many people looked back with nostalgia to the Empire and despised Weimar politicians as jumped-up nobodies, while the Communists and National Socialists hated the liberals more than they hated each other. 'Progressive' intellectuals played a discreditable role. By one-sided ridicule of the Republic and *Spiessbürgertum*, writers like Tucholsky played into the hands of the Republic's totalitarian enemies. Even so, it is likely that the Republic would have survived, had it not been for the depression of the early 1930s, in which unemployment rose to twenty per cent.

The obvious inability of the Brüning Government to tackle unemployment led to a revival of support for the N.S.D.A.P. (*Nazionalsozialistische Deutsche Arbeiter-Partei*) and to their obtaining a majority of seats in Parliament. The Hitler Government – constitutionally elected – then proceeded to overthrow the Republic and gain unfettered power.

The National Socialist government was socialistic, in the sense that it extended state control over all aspects of the economy. Wages, prices and rents were frozen, and the increased production, as Germany moved out of the depression, channelled

[1] Quoted in Kohn, *The Mind of Germany*, p. 17.

into military production, or quasi-military purposes such as the construction of motorways. When prices and rents are frozen for long periods, the market mechanism for allocating resources is put out of action, and it is necessary to introduce a system of centralised administrative control (*Zentralverwaltungs-wirtschaft*). And if prices (including rents) are held substantially below the costs of production, supply tends to dry up – as has often happened as a result of rent control. In fact the Nazi regime developed an elaborate system of administrative control, and very few houses were built during this period. The policy of increased public spending on armaments helped to overcome the depression – although recovery was very little quicker than in the United Kingdom or the United States. In general however the economic efficiency of the Nazi system of centralised control did not compare particularly favourably with German achievements either before or since.

The Federal Republic

After 1945 West Germany had suffered the traumatic experiences of the Nazi regime and the war, but was also faced with appalling economic problems. Her cities were in ruins; the country had been cut in two along the main lines of communication; there were millions of homeless refugees. After the initial shock, and the struggle to restore the basic services of civilised life, it became clear that the country was faced with a task not only of physical but also of moral reconstruction. It was necessary to think out political, economic and social policies afresh, reaching back to pre-Nazi traditions but re-interpreting them in the light of modern conditions.

The outcome was a new inter-nationalism in international relations and a revival of liberalism in economic and social affairs. The Nazi experience made people conscious of the defects of a completely planned and centralised economic system. There was therefore considerable appeal in the market system, because of the way in which it decentralises decision-making. In reports on economic policy written just after the war, one frequently finds arguments that a market economy enables people to be independent and self-respecting, instead of always having to crawl before some petty official to obtain a permit.

Social Market Economy

The outcome was a consensus philosophy in the late 1950s and 1960s which is most conveniently summed up in the phrase *soziale Marktwirtschaft*, perhaps best translated as 'socially responsible market economy', although I will use the literal translation for convenience. The phrase, coined by Professor A. Müller-Armack, was associated mainly with Ludwig Erhard as Economics Minister in the Adenauer Governments, and was for a time associated with the Christian Democrats, where policies differed from the 'clause four' type of socialism at first advocated by the Social Democrats. However in the 'Godesberg Programme' of 1959, the Social Democrats abandoned Marxism and embraced very similar ideas. In subsequent years, Professor Karl Schiller – the party's most distinguished economic theorist – introduced more economic sophistication into the concept of the 'social market economy' and – as Economics Minister after 1956 – implemented policies which complemented those of Erhard.

It would of course be wrong to assume that every policy adopted in the Federal Republic has been the result of a clearly thought-out philosophy. However the German character is inclined to seek a general philosophical basis for specific policies, as any British reader of German newspapers will soon realise, and the concept of the 'social market economy' has played an important role in West German affairs. The concept was introduced by Ludwig Erhard and became the slogan of the Christian Democrats. The concept, if not the term, was accepted by the Social Democrats in the Godesberg Programme and given a more modern economic content by Professor Schiller. In the early 1970s the Social Democrats began to swing back to a more *dirigiste* and Marxist philosophy (hence the retirement of Professor Schiller) but many other people were beginning to talk of the need to re-interpret the concept.

It can be argued that the term is a mere slogan, with no precise meaning. It has certainly been somewhat different things to different men, but it is a useful description for a range in the spectrum of economic and social policy. There were genuine differences of policy between Ludwig Erhard and the S.P.D. in 1949, or between Professor Schiller and his S.P.D. cabinet colleagues in 1972; the views of Erhard and Schiller, although not identical, can be usefully indicated by the term 'social market economy'.

The philosophy of the 'social market economy' derived from several streams of thought, different combinations of which can produce somewhat different interpretations. Four in particular may be mentioned: the modern neo-liberal and 'Keynesian' schools of economics; liberal social and political theory; Catholic social teaching; the tradition of local self-government.

One of the most influential economists was Walter Eucken (1891–1950), founder of the 'Freiburg School' of market-orientated economics. His most influential work _Grundsätze der Wirtschaftspolitik_ was published posthumously in 1952.[1] His ideas have been developed by several other economists, including Professor Schiller.[2] Although these writers can, to some extent, be considered as interpreters of modern Anglo-Saxon thought, they did add some new concepts. They stressed that specific policies should be viewed in the context of the economic system as a whole. It is a besetting sin of politicians (and journalists) faced with a particular problem – for example, rising rents, or a disturbingly large inflow of speculative foreign capital, to name only two recent problems – to wish to 'do something' irrespective of the effects of _ad hoc_ measures in the longer term, or on other aspects of the problem. The economists stressed that there are basically two ways of managing an economy, or a sector of an economy; the market mechanism, or a centrally planned system. A well-functioning market system can satisfy the multifarious individuals' demands of individuals effectively, and the economists made the value judgements that it was individuals who mattered. It is also, on past experience, compatible with political democracy, which a centrally planned system for the whole economy has not shown itself to be. A centrally planned economy is efficient in concentrating resources when there is one overriding aim – such as winning a war – but its efficiency is lower than that of a well-functioning market economy when there is no such overriding aim. A centrally

---

[1] Better known in the U.K. and U.S.A. is Professor F. A. Hayek, _The Road to Serfdom_ (1940) and the _Constitution of Liberty_ (1960) whose approach is similar.
[2] See his excellent short article on 'Wirtschaftspolitik' in _Handwörterbuch der sozialen Wissenschaften_.

planned system can be defended as a means of overcoming the effects of income differences, and giving everyone an equal chance. But privileges of status, for the controllers of the economy, then take the place of privilege based on wealth. Thus the economists favoured a market economy, and believed that it could operate in most fields of the economy. However only the most extreme neo-liberals denied that there were fields in which a centrally planned system was necessary. Hardly anyone in West Germany seriously suggested that the old-established system of state education should be replaced by private schools.

But even a market economy requires a framework within which to operate, and the creation of this framework is the responsibility of the state. There is need for an anti-monopoly policy, not only in the traditional 'trust-busting' sense but – perhaps more importantly – through opening up the home market to foreign competition, providing tax and legal systems which enable small firms to expand, and encourage a variety of types of enterprise, for example, co-operatives as against privately-owned firms. Moreover, as in any other game, there have to be rules for competition. If consumers are to make their purchases rationally, it has to be ensured that those who take part in the competitive process are properly qualified, that company accounts are properly scrutinised, that quality and standardising controls are enforced, shopkeepers forced to display prices etc. (In most of these fields, in fact, West Germany has gone further than the United Kingdom or France.) This type of rule-setting is termed by Professor Schiller 'influencing the market' (*Marktbeeinflussungen*) and he draws the useful contrast with 'intervention' and 'control' of the market (*Markt-interventionen, Marktregulierungen*). When the state intervenes in the market, it alters the data on which the participants work, and so changes the outcome, without altering the process: for example, a (moderate) tariff on imports will reduce imports, while still leaving buyers free to buy them. Regulation of the market, on the other hand, refers to methods such as price controls, rationing or quotas, which prevent the normal working of the market; except as temporary measures they necessitate the introduction of further controls, and eventually the substitution of a centrally planned system.

A similar useful distinction is that between procedures which are consistent with the market system (*marktkonform*) and those that are not. For example, if it is desired to lower the cost of housing for poor people, the payment of a housing allowance is consistent with a free market in housing, whereas rent control is not. Similarly, it could be argued – although here the case is less clear-cut – that the arrangements in force in early 1972 to discourage the inflow of capital into West Germany by, in effect, taxing the returns from it, were consistent with an international capital market, whereas the restrictions then introduced on the purchase of German securities were not. (This, at least, was the view of Professor Schiller, and the immediate cause of his resignation.) However it is not always possible to put policy measures neatly into one category or the other; for example, some degree of progressive taxation is consistent with a market economy, but when marginal rates reach very high levels they can begin to affect 'incentive'.

The same reasoning can be used in a broader sense to distinguish between policies which are consistent with any economic system (*systemkonform*) and those which are not. This approach can be used to assess modifications to sectors – such as education or town planning – which even in West Germany are organised on the basis of centralised planning. This concept helps to concentrate attention on the defects of *ad hoc* policies. If a deliberate decision is made to substitute a centrally planned for a market system, or vice versa, well and good. What needs to be avoided is a series of isolated measures which undermine the system, without this being intended. All of which has a moral for the present state of West Germany, as well as for more 'pragmatic' countries.

The 'Freiburg School' was weak on macro-economics (i.e. the control of broad aggregates such as unemployment or the price level). It tended to assume that a neutral monetary policy would assure the avoidance of booms and slumps, and had not taken much account of 'Keynesian' developments in economic thought. Professor Schiller incorporated these ideas into the analysis of the Freiburg School, stressing that policies were needed to stabilise the economy, but that these should take the form of global guidance (*globale Steuerung*), i.e. influencing aggregates such as consumption and investment, through such general measures as budget surpluses and deficits, changes in the money supply, or exchange rate adjustments, rather than through specific, physical interventions, such as encouraging or prohibiting a particular investment project.

Professor Schiller has summed up his approach as follows:

> Globale Massnahmen haben grundsätzlich den Vorzug vor punktuellen Eingriffen; bei mikroökonomischen Problemen entscheide im Zweifelsfalle die Konkurrenz! Erscheinen aber mikropolitische Massnahmen unumgänglich, so sind Markt-beeinflussungen and -interventionen wiederum den Markt-regulierungen vorzuziehen.[1]

'Social' Influences

But the philosophy of the 'social market economy' was not derived solely from economics. The coiner of the phrase, Professor A. Müller-Armack, has always stressed that the market mechanism is only part of his philosophy. As he puts it in an article published in English:

> It is wrong to regard the Social Market Economy merely as a variety of neo-liberalism. – Whereas neo-liberalism regards the machinery of competition as the sole principle of organisation, the concept of the Social Market Economy has grown from different roots. These lie in dynamic theory and in social anthropology, both of which were developed in the 1920s under a different view of the State and a development of the concept of a way of life that was largely rejected by neo-liberalism.[2]

What he seems to be saying is that individuals are not merely isolated consumers in a market system, but are also members of social, economic and political groups whose interests need to be represented and reconciled, with as much devolution of decision-making as possible. The emphasis on small groups, somewhere between the individual and the nation, is characteristically German, and contrasts with the tendency of British economists

[1] 'Wirtschaftspolitik', in *Handwörterbuch*, p. 215.
[2] 'The Social Market Economy', in *The German Economic Review* (1965), vol. 3, no. 2. See also his short article in the *Handwörterbuch der sozialen Wissenschaften* and the article under the same heading in *Staatslexikon* (Herder Verlag).

and political scientists to assume that the only important *foci* of attention are the individual, the firm and the government.[1] This emphasis on small groupings is reflected in the growth of the co-operative movement, particularly in the fields of housing and distribution, in the very decentralised system of local government, and in many aspects of semi-public administration, such as the *Kammern* (chambers) in trade, industry and agriculture which control matters such as industrial training.

Professor A. Müller-Armack has also stressed the need to complement the market system with various 'social' policies; to assist the old, the ill, the handicapped, the disabled, the unemployed; to ease the transition in industries – such as agriculture – in which rapid structural changes are taking place; to provide education which will enable people to cope with social and technological change; to deal with problems, such as town planning, which the market, by itself, cannot solve.

In the implementation of a 'social market economy' there were two influences which encouraged the 'social' and tended to offset the purely 'market' approach – Catholic social teaching and the strong tradition of local government. Modern Catholic social teaching, which has been more progressive in Germany than in many other countries, has stressed that the worker is not simply a hand, who is entitled merely to his wages, but that, through his labour, he contributes just as much to the enterprise as does the employer through his capital and management, and is therefore entitled to security and some measure of participation in running the business. This theory has contributed to the arrangements for co-direction and joint consultation in industry. (But there is a divergence of views here, which has become apparent in recent discussions on *Mitbestimmung*. The interests of the employees in a firm can – beyond a certain point – clash with the requirement to serve the market, i.e. the consumers.)

Another influence has been the strong tradition of state and

---

[1] Lord Keynes however once expressed the same idea: 'I believe that in many cases the ideal size for the unit of control and organisation lies somewhere between the individual and the modern State. I suggest, therefore, that progress lies in the growth and the recognition of semi-autonomous bodies within the State – bodies whose criterion of action within their own field is solely the public good as they understand it, and from whose deliberations motives of private advantage are excluded. . . .' 'The End of Laissez-Faire' in *Essays in Persuasion*.

town government, going back to the Middle Ages. Regional and municipal autonomy, suppressed but not destroyed by the Nazi regime, has been encouraged in the Federal Republic. Nothing could be more erroneous than to regard the extensive administrative devolution in the Federal Republic as 'an idea wished on the Germans by their allied conquerors'.[1] The principle of regional devolution of authority is well founded in German history; even the Empire of 1871 was a federal state, in spite of the dominance of Prussia. Moreover the German towns have traditionally exercised administrative powers. Thus whereas several unacceptable ideas which the Allies sought to impose on the Federal Republic were repealed, the main powers of the *Länder* and the municipalities have remained. There are some who think that federalism has been carried too far in some fields, but the principle is generally accepted that power should rest with the *Gemeinde*, unless it can clearly be shown that it should not rest with the *Land*, and that it should rest with the *Land*, unless it can be clearly shown that it is a matter for the federal government.

The bundle of principles which came to be known by the term 'social market economy' did not always represent a clear-cut and distinctive philosophy. Nevertheless they strongly influenced many of the policies initiated in the early years of the Federal Republic. The removal of controls after the currency reform of 1948 was primarily the result of Dr Erhard's belief in a market economy, and was taken in the face of strong criticism by the British and French authorities. Similarly, in the fields of industrial relations and housing policy, ideas of 'social market economy' led to markedly different policies than those adopted in the United Kingdom or France.

On the other hand, none of the proponents of the 'social market economy' developed any distinctive approach to social security or education. These shared in West Germany's rising prosperity, but in both cases institutions dating back to the time of Weimar and the Empire were refurbished. One old institution – the University – eventually collapsed, and as a result of a superficial analysis of the problem, new policies of an extremely dubious kind were adopted. It is therefore impossible to explain all aspects of West German economic and social life in terms of

[1] A. Shonfield, *Modern Capitalism*, p. 273.

'social market economy', but the question of what it meant, and where it stands today, may help to give coherence to the discussion of many aspects of economic policy. On other matters – such as education – the general principles involved are peculiar to the particular topic, although largely applicable in any developed country.

READING

Alfred Grosser, *Deutschlandbilanz: Geschichte Deutschlands seit 1945.* (Munich: Hanser Verlag, 1970).

Hajo Holborn, *A History of Modern Germany*, 3 vols (Knopf, 1959).

Karl Kaiser and Roger Morgan (eds) *Britain and West Germany* (O.U.P., 1971).

3 Growth and Structure of the West German Economy

The area which now forms the Federal Republic had in 1939 a fairly high standard of living, highly developed industries, especially in the metal-working and chemical fields, a skilled industrial labour force, well-run and pleasant cities, and a structurally backward agriculture which had not undergone an enclosure movement. After the war a fifth of the housing stock had been destroyed, the standard of living had sunk to a subsistence level, several million women had been widowed, while at the same time millions of refugees were flowing in from the East. Thus the West German economy had first to recover from the effects of the war, and provide homes and jobs for the increased population. After this had been achieved, real income went on increasing to levels well above those achieved before the war. This led to the type of changes in private and public demand and industrial structure which have characterised all affluent societies.

Population

First, the population changes. Some 10 million Germans were expelled from the area beyond the Oder and Neisse and other countries, and several million fled from the Soviet zone; the inflow continued at a lower level until the building of the Berlin Wall in 1961. The net population changes between 1939 and 1960 have been estimated as follows: war losses of 2·3 million, together with an influx of 13·4 million and a natural increase of 2·5 million, giving a net increase of 13·6 million.[1] The influx of Germans from the East was the biggest population movement in Germany since the tribal wanderings of the fourth–sixth century. There is not a town, and scarcely a village, in West Germany which does not contain a proportion of Germans

[1] *Germany Reports* (Press and Information Office of the Federal Republic, 1966).

born in the East. The resettling of the refugees was assisted, in the early days, by a range of subsidies, but it depended predominantly on personal initiative. It has succeeded – both economically, socially and politically – to such an extent that the problem of the 'expellees' is hardly discussed any longer.

During the 1950s, the working population rose with the rise in total population and the reduction in unemployment. It has since levelled off at around 27 million. A high proportion of women are employed; there are some 10 million working women as against 17 million men. In the 1960s a new type of worker appeared on the scene – the immigrant worker (*Gastarbeiter*). These came from the Mediterranean countries where jobs were less readily available, at first Italy and later Spain, Greece and Turkey. In 1972 there were $2\frac{1}{4}$ million *Gastarbeiter* in the Federal Republic. Italy is in the Common Market, so that – theoretically at least – there is free entry for Italian workers. Workers from the other countries are admitted only on work permits, for a year at a time. The *Gastarbeiter* have been useful in industry – the Turks have a particularly good reputation for industriousness – but they have not been integrated into German society. They tend to live together, often in crowded conditions, and to spend their free time together. Groups of swarthy men can often be seen standing around talking in the spacious entrance halls of German railway stations – probably the nearest thing to the sunny streets of their homeland.

The need for immigrant workers arose for two reasons – a general labour shortage caused by the pace of industrial growth, and a specific shortage in certain unattractive jobs, such as refuse collection. So far, government and industrial leaders have treated the presence of the *Gastarbeiter* as wholly desirable, using the same economic arguments that have been used to justify Commonwealth immigration in Britain – that the immigrants do dirty and low-paid jobs that the Germans don't want to do. Hardly anyone has posed the question whether a society resting on a despised helot class is desirable or, in the long run, tolerable. But a few voices – the *Frankfurter Allgemeine* paper being one – are beginning to pose this question.

The industrial distribution of the labour force has changed over time (table 17). There is the familiar tendency for service

Table 16

POPULATION OF THE FEDERAL REPUBLIC
(million)

	Total population	Working population	Foreign workers
1939	43·0		
1950	50·4	20·4	—
1960	55·4	26·2	0·3
1965	59·3	27·2	1·2
1970	61·0	27·2	1·9

Source: All tables in this chapter, unless otherwise stated are from the *Statistisches Jahrbuch* or *20 Jahre Leistung in Zahlen*, Bundesministerium für Wirtschaft und Finanzen, 1971.

Table 17

WORKING POPULATION ACCORDING TO INDUSTRY
(million)

	1950	1960	1965	1970
Agriculture, forestry	5·0	3·6	3·0	2·4
Manufacturing industry	8·7	12·5	13·2	13·2
Trade and transport	2·9	4·5	4·8	4·8
Service industries	}3·8	3·3	3·7	4·1
State employees, and miscellaneous		2·3	2·5	2·7
	20·4	26·2	27·2	27·2

industries to grow as income rises, but the most striking change has been the rapid fall in the agricultural labour force – which has lost over 2½ million workers since 1950. This is a world wide trend, but it has been particularly rapid in the Federal Republic because an obsolete agricultural sctructure, with very small farms, has been subjected to the pressures of a very efficient and dynamic industrial sector. Agriculture has been the most difficult 'problem industry' in the Federal Republic, as discussed in the next chapter.

National Income

Many indications of the economic changes in a country can be obtained from the national income figures. National income per head, in real terms (i.e. discounting price rises) has risen since

1950 by rates normally of between 3 and 6%, with a check only in the slight recession of 1966/7.

The distribution of income between income from employment, from property (bonds, houses) and from trading (corporation profits and income of self-employed persons) is shown in table 18. Trading profits have fallen as a percentage of national income (from 37% in 1960 to 25% in 1971), and have barely risen in real terms since 1960. However, together with sub-

Table 18

DISTRIBUTION OF NATIONAL INCOME*
(000 million **D.M.**)

	Income from employment	Income from property	Trading profits and income	Total
1950				75
1960	143	6	87	236
1965	230	14	111	355
1966	248	18	112	378
1967	248	20	108	376
1968	266	23	128	417
1969	300	26	133	459
1970	353	34	140	527
1971	400	37	143	580

Source: *Deutsches Industrieinstitut.*

*Net national product at factor cost, and current prices.

stantial savings by individuals and the state, they have been sufficient to finance a high total rate of investment – around 25% of national income in the 1960s (table 19).

The Germans have shown a high propensity to save: the proportion of personal income saved has risen steadily since

Table 19

UTILISATION OF NATIONAL INCOME
(per cent)

	Private consumption	Public consumption	Investment	Balancing item*	
1950	64·7	14·3	18·5	2·5	100
1960	57·0	13·6	24·0	5·4	100
1971	54·3	17·0	26·8	1·9	100

* External balance and stock changes.

1949, and was 12·4% in 1970. The total savings in the economy are now divided fairly evenly between individuals, corporations and the state (table 20). The rising level of personal savings is also reflected in firms' methods of financing new investment; the proportion financed by outside capital has risen steadily to 58% in 1970.

Table 20

TOTAL SAVINGS

	Total (000 million **D.M.**)	*Individuals*	*Corporations* (per cent)	*State*
1950	9·8	20·0	24·3	55·7
1960	59·4	25·7	43·5	30·8
1970	116·6	38·9	31·8	29·3

The growth of personal income since the hungry postwar years led to various 'waves' of consumption. In the early 1950s people spent most of their extra money on food (*Fresswelle*). When they were once again eating fairly well they turned to clothing, housing and then services like travel (*Wohnwelle*,

Table 21

CONSUMPTION PER HEAD PER YEAR

	Beef and pork (kilograms)	*Coffee*	*Tea*	*Beer* (litres)	*Wine*	*Cigarettes* (number)
1952	32	0·6	0·05	65	8	784
1960	48	2·9	0·11	120	13	1614
1970	58	4·0	0·15	182	16	2514

Table 22

PRICES AND WAGES
(1950 = 100)

	Retail prices	*Hourly wages in manufacturing*	
		Nominal	*Real**
1950	100	100	100
1960	121	209	174
1965	138	329	237
1970	157	469	299

* i.e. after allowing for price rises.

Table 23

AVERAGE EXPENDITURE OF 4-PERSON WAGE-EARNING HOUSEHOLDS WITH AVERAGE INCOME

	Total D.M.	Food, drink, tobacco	Clothing	Housing	Domestic expenses %	Transport	Sport, Education, Entertainment	Other
1960	607	45·3	12·6	10·5	14·6	5·0	9·9	2·1
1965	881	40·0	11·9	11·2	14·5	9·7	9·9	2·8
1970	1089	35·3	10·8	15·5	13·7	10·8	10·9	3·0

Reisewelle etc.). In recent years, it is noticeable that the proportion of family income spent on food and drink has fallen, whereas the proportion spent on housing has risen. The increased expenditure on housing is partly because housing has become dearer in relation to other goods, but also because consumers have chosen to buy (or rent) bigger and better houses.

The Public Sector

Roughly one third of national income is taken in taxation (and compulsory social insurance contributions). The proportion has remained fairly constant, although with a slight upward trend in the 1960s arising from the growth, in particular, of the cost of defence and social security; the figure was 31·5 in 1960 and 33·4 in 1971. In the early 1960s, the West German figure was high by comparison with other European countries, but since then the percentages in other countries have risen even faster, so that the German percentage is now slightly lower than in most West European countries.

The allocation of public funds is intricately involved with the division of authority amongst the three tiers of government – federal, provincial and local. Whether the West German system is described as federal, or unitary with extensive devolution of power, is a matter of semantics. The important thing is that considerable power is given to the provinces, or states (*Länder*), and to the communities, or local authorities (*Gemeinden*). The federal government is responsible for foreign affairs, defence, general economic policy, main roads and railways, social security. The *Länder* are responsible for police, education and a great deal of internal administration; the local authorities are free to undertake all local matters not taken over by the federal or provincial governments. Real power exists only when the provincial and local authorities have an independent source of finance, but the German experience shows that this does not necessarily have to consist of a completely separate system of taxation. Provided that the provincial and local governments are guaranteed by law a percentage share in the yield of national taxes, they retain their financial independence.

The arrangements for the division of tax receipts were laid down in the West German constitution (*Grundgesetz*) but were extensively modified in 1969. The most important taxes – income tax, corporation tax and value-added tax – are divided between the federal and *Länder* governments. The federal government receives half the yield from the income and corporation tax, the other half goes to the *Länder*, with a periodically adjusted proportion going to the local authorities. Other taxes are reserved either for the federal, *Länder* or local governments. The *Länder* governments receive the wealth tax, death duties, vehicle licences and the tax on beer. The federal government receives other taxes, apart from the land tax and the business tax (*Gewerbesteuer*). These two taxes are levied on an assessed value of land and businesses, and are comparable to British

Table 24

RECEIPTS OF MAIN TAXES 1971
(000 million D.M.)

Income tax	70·4
Corporation tax	7·1
Value-added tax	30·9
Petrol tax	12·4
Tobacco tax	6·9
Business tax	12·3
Other taxes	32·2
Total tax receipts	172·2

'rates'. The local authorities can – within limits – vary the tax rates, according to their needs. Until 1969 the local authorities were solely dependent on these taxes but were given a share of the receipts from income tax to avoid the problems of relying exclusively on this inelastic tax base.

The most interesting thing about these arrangements is that they show how a decentralised administrative system can be financed. Some taxes can be reserved for regional authorities, but it is also possible to allocate national taxes in agreed

Table 25

PLANNED EXPENDITURE 1972
(000 million D.M.)

Bund	Länder	Gemeinden
111	82	44

proportions. This system of allowing tax revenues enables the *Länder* and *Gemeinden* to retain the independence which so impresses visitors from countries with more centralised systems.

Table 26

PUBLIC EXPENDITURE (FEDERAL, PROVINCIAL AND LOCAL)
(000 million D.M.)

	1950	*1961*	*1970*
Defence	4·7	12·2	20·5
Law and order	1·1	3·7	7·9
Schools	1·7	6·6	18·5
Universities and research	0·4	2·4	9·8
Social security	7·5	24·3	40·3
Health and recreation	1·0	3·8	10·3
Housing and environment	3·5	7·9	11·0
Industry (including agriculture)	1·9	6·2	14·5
Roads and transport	1·3	6·9	17·2
Total (including miscellaneous)	27·9	95·3	196·4

Foreign Trade

In 1950 West Germany exported a mere D.M. 8·4 milliard (000 million) and imported D.M. 11·4 milliard. Thereafter both rose sharply and uninterruptedly to D.M. 125 and 110 milliard respectively in 1970. The surplus on the 'visible' account has been partly balanced by a deficit on invisibles (5·3 milliard on tourism alone) and by remittances home by foreign workers (4·5 milliard).

At times however there have been embarrassing surpluses on the balance of payments, and this has prompted the idea that these could be eliminated by encouraging German firms to invest abroad. Investment abroad has been viewed favourably by all governments and – like investment in West Germany from abroad – has been free from controls. Some investment has taken place, and has increased sharply since the mid-1960s. However the capital outflow has been fairly evenly matched by capital inflows; by 1970, both stood at a total of D.M. 21 milliard. The biggest direct investment in West Germany has been by the American-based 'multi-national' firms such as General Motors and Ford. A number of German firms have invested abroad. Volkswagen, for example, has set up a plant in Brazil. But many firms have perhaps been inhibited by the loss of foreign investments in two world wars, and many German firms do not yet possess the venturesomeness and international approach of the American 'multi-national' firms.

Germany's return to world markets was achieved partly by her traditional industries – steel products, chemicals, optical equipment – but even more by new products – cars, radios, electronic equipment – often produced by new firms like Volkswagen or Grundig. As incomes rose, home demand increased for imported goods, as well as 'invisible' imports such as travel; the result has been a change in the pattern of imports. Germany had traditionally imported food and raw materials. With rising prosperity, imports of manufactured goods began to account for an increasing proportion of imports – now over half.

Exports – primarily of manufactured products – have been mainly to the developed countries of Western Europe and North America, the largest markets being France, the Netherlands, the United States and Italy, although there are some exports to most countries. Many German businessmen have hopes of increasing exports to the Communist bloc, but exports to these countries make up only around 4% of total exports. Exports to the German Democratic Republic (always shown separately in the statistics as 'inner-German trade') amount to around 2% of exports.

One of the greatest success stories of West German exporting was the Volkswagen 'beetle'. Starting with no export experience at all, Volkswagen built up the world's largest export of a single model, on the basis of a robust, well-made product with excellent servicing. But Volkswagen also illustrates the change that has come over world markets since those early days. With the increased competition of Japanese cars, the gradual obsolescence of the 'beetle', and the difficulty of introducing a radically different model, Volkswagen has run into severe financial difficulties, from which it has not yet emerged.

Not only has exporting become more difficult. Imports from low-wage countries have increasingly challenged, and even supplanted, the production of many goods in Germany itself. Nearly all radios, tape recorders and black-and-white televisions are now imported, and the famous firm of Zeiss Ikon has had to suspend the production of amateur cameras. This is a development foreseen many years ago by Dr Ludwig Erhard, who forecast that in time many less sophisticated products would be better produced in the developing countries. Some German firms have accepted this trend. Rollei have transferred their entire production of cameras to Singapore, thus escaping the fate of Zeiss Ikon, while others have arranged for production under licence by Japanese firms. This development is an extremely promising one for the developing countries; it could also benefit Germany, if German producers switch to more sophisticated products. But this switch requires retraining and a rising level of technical skill. The problems involved are at present being surmounted, but if they became too severe there could conceivably be a resurgence of protectionist feeling.

The Structure of German Industry

German industry and commerce in many ways has the same characteristics and problems as industry and commerce in any other industrial country. There are however some peculiarities which deserve mention, among them the organisation of the banking system, the strength of the co-operative system in distribution and the special problems of agriculture.

The 25 largest German companies in manufacturing industries are listed in table 27. This however is somewhat misleading, for it excludes both nationalised industries such as the railways and post, and also some important co-operative or trade-union owned organisations. *Neue Heimat*, the building firm owned by the trade unions, has a turnover of D.M. 3·4 milliard (000 m.).

In recent years there have been a number of mergers, and this has given rise to discussion as to how much competition remains, and how far therefore the 'social market economy' can be relied on. Yet in fact – as in other countries – it is extremely difficult to show that there has been a rise in the degree of concentration over a substantial period of time. In some industries there are clearly fewer firms than in the 1950s or 1920s, but on the other hand new firms in new industries have been formed. Moreover the interwar period was one in which cartels and trusts were actively supported by the government, and in which competition from imports was limited.

In most branches of German industry today there is intensive competition, between both German and foreign firms, even

Table 27

THE 25 LARGEST GERMAN COMPANIES IN MANUFACTURING INDUSTRY

	Turnover (000 million D.M.)	Employees (000)
Volkswagenwerk	15·8	190
Siemens	11·7	300
Farbwerke Hoechst	11·1	139
Daimler-Benz	11·0	144
August Thyssen-Hütte	10·8	97
Badische Anilin- u. Sodafabrik	10·5	107
Farbenfabriken Bayer	9·2	102
AEG-Telefunken	8·5	178
Mannesmann	6·5	76
Krupp-Konzern	6·0	80
Robert Bosch	5·5	117
Hoesch	5·2	64
Metallgesellschaft	5·1	36
Rheinstahl	4·8	71
Gutehoffnungshütte	4·7	68
Salzgitter	2·9	29
Gelsenberg	2·7	13
Klöckner-Humboldt-Deutz	2·4	47
Buderus'sche Eisenwerke	2·3	35
Feldmühle-Dynamit-Nobel	2·2	31
Klöckner-Werke	2·2	31
Degussa	2·0	15
Agfa-Gevaert-Gruppe	1·9	34
B.M.W.	1·7	23
Varta	1·6	27

Source: *The Fortune Directory.*

though the number of firms may be small. It cannot plausibly be argued that 'workable' competition does not prevail.

The Banking System

The Federal Republic, like most other countries, has a central bank and a range of different types of commercial bank. The central bank, the *Deutsche Bundesbank*, controls the money supply and supervises the operations of commercial banks. It has to obey general directives from the Government, but has considerable independence in putting forward its views on monetary and economic policy in general. In the early part of 1972, for example, the *Bundesbank* came out in favour of controls on speculative capital inflows, to which the Economics and Finance Minister, Professor Schiller, was opposed. Indeed, the Bank President, who attends Cabinet meetings, was involved in the manœuvrings which goaded Professor Schiller into resignation.

The commercial banks fall into several categories. The banking transactions of the 'little man' are mainly handled by the *Sparkassen* ('savings banks'), the co-operative banks and the Post Office Giro. The *Sparkassen* are public corporations, linked with local authorities and undertaking banking work for them, but also taking deposits from the public. The co-operative savings banks are strongest in rural areas, often consisting of a small department in a village trading co-operative. Nearly everyone has a *Sparbuch* – in 1969, to be precise, 90% of wage earners and 95% of salary-earners. Another type of savings bank which has expanded enormously under the Federal Republic is the *Bausparkasse*. This provides savings schemes for house purchase, which are subsidised by the government.

The *Kreditbanken*, on the other hand, are large national companies, with far fewer branches than the *Sparkassen*, and fewer depositors, but larger total balances. They deal primarily in large sums, and are a major source of finance for industry. In this respect they are more like British 'merchant banks' than the British 'big five' banks. There are also banks which specialise in issuing bonds for public authorities.

Savings by individuals have risen sharply since the 1950s, and amounted to 38·9% of total savings in 1970. A large proportion of them are used to finance industry, but indirectly through the banks rather than directly through the purchase of shares, or unit trusts, which have not become a popular form of investment. There was a tendency in the 1960s to invest in shares, and a lot of hopeful Germans invested in Investors' Overseas Services, the creation of Mr Bernie ('you too can be rich') Cornfield; the subsequent *débâcle* did nothing to popularise shareownership. (But even the shares of reputable companies have not – since 1960 – proved a very good investment: the index of share prices has remained virtually unchanged, with a net yield of around 3%.) Ownership of other forms of capital has however spread rapidly. A sample survey has given the following figures for various categories of household.

Table 28

AVERAGE CAPITAL OF PRIVATE HOUSEHOLDS 1969
D.M.

	Savings*	Life Insurance (Capital sum)	Securities	Houses and Land
Wage-earners	4510	6220	380	10,120
Salary-earners	7270	14,970	2290	11,630
Civil servants	7550	8440	1660	14,760
Self-employed (including farmers)	9090	24,180	1470	49,420
All households	4990	8820	1630	16,610

Source: Professor Willgerodt, '*Vermögen für alle*' (Düsseldorf, 1971).

* In *Sparkassen* and *Bausparkassen*.

The need to encourage widespread property ownership was stressed by the advocates of a 'social market economy', and various savings schemes have been directly or indirectly sub-sidised by the federal government. One of the most important was the 1961 'Act for the Encouragement of Ownership of Property by Employees'. This granted tax concessions when an employer sets up a scheme for paying a sum to each employee's account, which has to be invested for five years. The statute is generally known as the '*624 D.M.-Gesetz*', from the yearly amount which now qualifies for tax relief. In 1971, 12 million workers were covered by schemes set up under it, and the total amount saved in that year was over D.M. 3000 million. In 1972 there was considerable discussion on further means of en-couraging '*Vermögensbildung*'. The trade unions have stressed that ownership of the means of production is concentrated in a few hands. In view however of the indirect method of financing German companies, it is necessary to distinguish between property in general and shareholding. It is true that effective control of the shareholding in most German companies is in the hands of a few persons, both large personal shareholders and – at least equally important – bankers who have invested funds deposited with them. But property in all forms – including indirect shareholding – has become much more widely distributed under the Federal Republic, and the process is continuing.

Co-operation

Another characteristic of the West German economic structure is the importance of co-operative forms of organisation. The postwar advocates of a market economy had laid considerable emphasis on the politically desirable dispersion of economic power. And this dispersion has indeed occurred, although its extent has been limited, much more than was realised in the early days of the Republic, by the modern need for large-scale production and distribution. Nevertheless in many industries the advantages of both size and smallness have been achieved by means of co-operation. This is particularly true in housing, agricultural marketing and retail distribution.

The important role of the housing associations is discussed below. The co-operative principle – in a wider sense than the consumer co-operative movement – has also played a most important role in retail distribution. In the retail grocery trade, in particular, there has been an organisational and technical revolution since the foundation of the Republic, but one in which the small private traders, by far-sighted co-operation, have to a large extent been able to maintain their position. In 1949 the grocery trade was mainly in the hands of independent and unorganised shopkeepers (as it still is in France). By 1964 the percentage of trade handled by independent shopkeepers had fallen to 6·3% while no less than 66·8% was in the hands of voluntary chains of various types, which provide the advantages of centralised buying while leaving the individual shops in private ownership. The formation of these voluntary chains has gone hand-in-hand with a changeover to self-service. Department stores and consumer co-operatives have expanded considerably, but the competitive position of the voluntary chains is now strong, and a large proportion of them should be able to hold their own.

Problems and Prospects

West German industry and commerce has been outstandingly successful in meeting the demands made upon it – in the early years for simple material goods, later for more sophisticated goods and services such as travel. It has also been remarkably successful in winning exports – at times embarrassingly so, although at present there is a reasonable balance in external payments (apart from short-term speculative movements). At the same time a large and well-planned programme of government expenditure has been very successful in supplying 'public' goods such as roads and public transport, public buildings and recreational facilities.

It seems clear however that in the future there will be even more emphasis on the environmental and social consequences of industrial production and technical change. West Germany's record in the environmental field is relatively good, but the problems of *Umweltschutz* have recently been widely discussed. A few steps in the right direction have already been taken – the halving of the lead content in petrol, the banning of flights over Germany by supersonic airliners – and many more are clearly on the way.

Similarly, more satisfying conditions of work, better public transport systems, better housing, will in future receive even higher priority than at present. Industry has already turned its attention to the technical problems, a great many civilising products are under development or in production – sunlight-reflecting glass to stop office workers being grilled, silent high speed magnetically-suspended trains, quieter lorries. At the same time there is likely to be increased emphasis on capital formation by wage earners, and on improving industrial relations at the works level.

There is however one social problem which is perhaps under-estimated. The West German economy has so far shown a tendency to invest at a level higher than that needed to give full employment to the indigenous labour force; the result has been the growth of an army of foreign workers. This alien and unassimilated body of workers doing unpopular jobs could well be a cause of serious social problems. One alternative would be to divert the surplus investment to investment in poorer countries, thus employing the *Gastarbeiter* at home, and stimulating economic development. This would probably be a socially preferable system. There is the danger of nationalistic opposition to foreign investment, although the objections can be reduced by arranging for a substantial degree of local participation, as Volkswagen and Rollei appear to have done in Brazil and Singapore. This type of investment could well offer one of the most promising ways in which West Germany, and other rich countries, could assist the economic development of the poorer countries.

READING

J. Hennessy and others, *Economic 'Miracles': studies in the resurgence of the French, German and Italian Economies since the Second World War* (André Deutsch, for the Institute of Economic Affairs, 1964).

G. Gutman and others, *Die Wirtschaftsverfassung der Bundesrepublik Deutschland* (Stuttgart: Gustav Fischer, 1964).

Ludwig Erhard, *Germany's Comeback in the World Market* ed. H. Gross (London, 1954).

Heinz Lampert, *Die Wirtschafts- und Sozialordnung der Bundesrepublik Deutschland* (Munich: Verlag G. Olzog, 1966).

4 West German Agriculture

The remarkable achievements of the Federal Republic of Germany in the industrial sector are well-known; the problems and achievements of West German agriculture are less well known. There is a widespread belief in Britain that West German farming is, as *The Economist* once put it, 'one of the most backward peasant communities in Europe'. This gives a false impression of the position. West German agriculture is technically quite advanced. The farm structure however is for the most part not adapted to modern needs. The consequent problems are particularly severe because a structurally outdated agriculture has, in the last decade, been subjected to the pressures of an advanced industrial economy.

The Historical Background

The present West German farm structure has an historical origin. Whereas in England, in the eighteenth century, large landowners laid out farms on more or less the pattern which exists today, this did not happen in those parts of Germany which now constitute the Federal Republic. At the beginning of the nineteenth century, the peasants finally acquired complete ownership of the land they cultivated, but this often consisted of scattered strips and blocks originating in the medieval open field system. One case has been reported in which a farmer owned fifty acres divided into 283 separate pieces! Moreover in those areas where Napoleon's *Code civil* had been adopted, the owner was obliged to divide his land equally amongst all his sons, which caused further fragmentation. The farmsteads were not – with some exception – scattered across the countryside in the middle of their land, like British farms, but were situated in the villages; in the tightly packed farmsteads people and animals lived in close proximity to each other, and the farmer travelled out to his fields.

A farm layout of this type is extremely inefficient, but is virtually impossible to alter without a concerted effort of farm consolidation (*Flurbereinigung*). Farmers have to be induced to exchange land with each other so that each obtains a single block of land, or at least several largish blocks. Spasmodic efforts were made in the nineteenth and early twentieth centuries to undertake consolidation, but no large scale programme was begun before the Second World War. In many parts of West Germany the typical agricultural layout still consists of a village of half-timbered farmsteads – picturesque and well-maintained but often not very satisfactory for living in – while around the village the countryside is divided up into narrow strips. The concentration of farmsteads in the villages may in the past have had social advantages. It was nevertheless inefficient, but this has only become a matter of urgency as agricultural labour has become scarcer and dearer in the 1950s and 1960s.

Together with this antiquated farm structure went, in the past, a somewhat low status of those who cultivated the land. This is summed up in the word *Bauer* (peasant) which, although associated with a good deal of romantic glorification of country life by German writers who generally lived in the town, also implied a horny-handed son of the soil. Only in recent years has the unemotional word *Landwirt* (farmer) begun to be adopted; the word itself reflects a changed status. The educational and social status of the farming population in what is now the Federal Republic was never as low as in, say, Italy or Southern France, and in the nineteenth century a great deal was done by men such as the co-operative pioneer *Reiffeisen* to improve social conditions in the villages, and by organisations such as the *Deutsche Landwirtschafts-Gesellschaft* to improve the techniques of farming. The nineteenth century also saw the development of the excellent agricultural schools, whose teachers also undertook advisory work, which have remained to this day. But the general educational level in the countryside was not raised to the level that was achieved in Denmark by the Folk High Schools.

When European agriculture came under pressure from the new lands of North America and Australasia at the end of the nineteenth century, Germany adopted a policy of protection, in which – largely as a result of the influence of the arable farmers in East Germany – the main emphasis was on the maintenance of the cereal price. Bismarck introduced an import tariff on cereals in 1879, and its level was raised by his successors. Although primarily designed to help the large cereal growers of the East, this policy of protection probably also benefited the whole of German agriculture in the short run, while at the same time possibly reducing the incentive to undertake structural reform such as was undertaken in Denmark.

Agricultural Policy since 1945

In the immediate postwar period, there was an extreme food shortage in Germany. Production in the Western zones had fallen to half the pre-war level, and supplies from the previously food-surplus Eastern areas were cut off. At the same time, the population of the Western zones was swollen by the influx of millions of refugees. Food rations in the period of 1945–7 averaged between 1200 and 1300 calories per head per day, about half the normally accepted minimum. In these circumstances, the wartime system of food control was naturally continued. But, as a result of a rapid recovery in production and a modest resumption of imports, it was possible to end rationing and government control of production and distribution in 1950.

The ending of control did not mean the ending of protection, any more than it did in Great Britain a few years later. There had already been a controversy on the future of German agricultural policy. The Freiburg School of neo-liberal economics opposed import quotas and any other type of physical intervention by the State, and looked forward to a re-integration of Germany in the world economy. It opposed regional groupings, but was prepared to accept a moderate import tariff, to compensate for distortions of competition on the world market for foodstuffs. The other view, which had its proponents mainly among practical men, favoured import controls, which it sought to show were not necessarily linked with a totalitarian political system, and looked forward to a regional European economic grouping as the first stage in the re-integration of Germany in the world economy.

The second view had, in the event, more influence on policy. The system introduced in 1950–1 was based on control of imports backed up by support buying, but – with some exceptions – leaving the internal market free. Thus an Import and

Storage Authority (which now implements Community policies) has maintained guaranteed prices by regulating imports, holding stocks, and being ready to intervene in buying cereals at the guaranteed price.

West German Agriculture in the Common Market

The Federal Republic's signature of the Treaty of Rome in 1957 was not opposed by the farming organisations, which shared the general feeling that this step was politically desirable. It soon became clear however that the implementation of a common agricultural policy would eventually involve problems for West German agriculture, as the Federal Republic had the highest level of agricultural producer prices, and it was unlikely that the guaranteed agricultural prices in the Community could be set at the German level.

These problems did not arise at once, since for some years after the signing of the Treaty of Rome only minor steps were taken to establish a common market for agricultural, as distinct from industrial, products. Some preferences were given to suppliers within the Community as against those outside it, but nothing was done to reduce the level of German guaranteed prices, symbolised by the 'key' cereal price. Indeed the Farmers Union maintained that it was implacably opposed to the slightest reduction in the cereal price, which made it very hard to see how any common agricultural market could be established. Even academic discussion of the possibility of a reduction in the cereal price was denounced, and after the publication in 1962 of a report by a group of experts, analysing the effects of a cereal price reduction, and the ways in which farmers could be compensated, local farmers drove into the University town of Göttingen on their tractors and demonstrated outside the departments of two professors of agricultural economics who had been on the committee.

In December 1964, after prolonged discussions in Brussels, and threats by France to block the progress of the Common Market in the industrial field unless comparable progress was made in the agricultural field, the Community's Council of Ministers reached agreement on the introduction of a common cereal price at the relatively high level of £37 a ton for wheat – a reduction of £4 from the German level. Shortly afterwards it was announced that German farmers would be compensated for the consequent loss of income by non-price subsidies paid on an acreage basis, and financed partly by the Community, partly by the German Exchequer.

The common prices for the Community are expressed in 'units of account', which are in fact United States dollars. Therefore when the Deutschmark was revalued in 1969 and 1971, the prices received by German farmers should have fallen correspondingly. The German government was unprepared to let this happen and obtained permission from Brussels to maintain Deutschmark prices by imposing 'temporary' levies on imports, even from other members of the Community. In this sense therefore there has been no common agricultural policy since 1969.

Decisions in Brussels have by no means eliminated national agricultural policies in West Germany or in other members of the Community. It is generally recognised in West Germany that the sweeping plans originally made – and still favoured – by the Brussels bureaucracy for a uniform agricultural policy from Schleswig-Holstein to Sicily were impracticable. But whereas some Germans favour an explicit 're-rationalising' of agricultural policy, others believe that this would open the door to un-co-ordinated and autarkic policies; they therefore favour a common, but flexible policy and this seems the most likely outcome.

On the general question of support for agriculture, opinions also differ. The traditional liberal view, held by some economists and put forward in some sections of the German press, is that price support delays structural change and keeps workers unproductively employed. Most West German agricultural economists take a somewhat more favourable view of a certain measure of income and price support. They point out that German agriculture is in a period of rapid change. Since the war two million people, roughly two-thirds of the labour force, have left agriculture for other occupations. At the same time, production has risen, and is now fifty per cent above the pre-war level (table 29). The movement of labour out of agriculture is, in percentage terms, the most rapid in any developed country since the war, and one of the most rapid that has ever occurred in any country. In these circumstances, it is improbable that the maintenance of prices above the level on the world market significantly slows down the rate of change in agriculture, although it prevents the extremely low incomes which would otherwise prevail.

Table 29

CHANGES IN AGRICULTURAL PRODUCTION: GERMAN FEDERAL REPUBLIC (AND CORRESPONDING PRE-1939 AREA)

	Food production in 'cereal units'* (million)	*Agricultural labour force* (*full-time man-units*) (1000)	*No. of holdings over 5 acres* (1000)
1935/38	33	3852	1355
1949/50	31	3885	1345
1960/1	49	2400	1120
1964/5	52	1918	1050
1970/71	59	1434	880

Source: *Statistisches Jahrbuch über Ernährung, Landwirtschaft und Forstwirtschaft.*

* The equivalent in crop or animal production of 1 ton of cereals.

Structural Reform

The movement out of agriculture has been mainly the pull of the booming industrial sector, but it has been supplemented in recent years by an explicit policy of structural reform. In the immediate postwar period, there was little interest in improving the antiquated layout of West German farms. Raising production was the main concern. Moreover, at this time the Farmers Union still held distinctly 'fundamentalist' ideas on agricultural policy, and there was a widespread feeling that it was a good thing to keep as many people as possible on the land. The situation was made worse by the presence of thousands of refugee farmers from the East, and the attempt to settle some of them on the land.

In the 1950s however the case for structural reform began to be increasingly accepted. The Agricultural Act of 1955 introduced a programme of financial aid for farm consolidation, and for social and 'infra-structure' investment in rural areas.

Under the 1955 Act, the federal government has to submit each year a report to the *Bundestag* examining agricultural incomes and comparing them with those of workers in 'comparable occupations'. The figures of 'comparable income' produced each year since 1955 show agricultural income as being about one-third below that in comparable occupations,

Table 30

INCOME IN AGRICULTURE* AND IN
'COMPARABLE OCCUPATIONS' IN INDUSTRY
(percentage difference)

| | *Size of farm (hectares)* | | |
	Under 20	*20–50*	*Over 50*
	%	%	%
1961/2	– 32	– 27	– 20
1964/5	– 31	– 16	+ 1
1968/9	– 26	– 18	– 3
1969/70	– 24	– 17	– 7

Source: *Agrarbericht 1972.*

* Full-time farms.

but rising at the same rate (table 30). Because of the problems of measuring agricultural income, the figures need to be viewed with considerable caution, but they nevertheless indicate that West German agriculture has, till now, been able on the whole to maintain a modest prosperity.

This 'Green Report' has to be accompanied by a 'Green Plan' indicating the sums that the government is planning to spend on agriculture in the coming year. These consist of aid for consolidation, various types of 'production' subsidies, such as those for fertilisers, subsidies for providing loans at low interest rates, and since 1963 payments for various social facilities in the countryside such as communal launderettes and cold stores (table 31). Consolidation has proved surprisingly expensive. It involves obtaining agreement among the farmers to exchange land among each other, and also lengthy and expensive surveying. Consolidation is generally accompanied by *Aussiedlung*, or the building of new farmsteads outside the village on the amalgamated land, which is also expensive.

Considerable progress has been made in consolidation, and throughout West Germany there are now many attractive new farmhouses standing in the middle of enclosed fields, which contrast sharply with the patchwork of strips where amalgamation has not taken place. Since the war, nine million acres have

Table 31

FEDERAL EXPENDITURE ON AGRICULTURE
(million D.M.)

	1956	1966	1971
Farm structure and investment aids	112	1611	1157
Pensions and insurance		730	935
Marketing		77	195
Price support		1442	3929
Other	318	240	647
Total	430	4100	6863

been consolidated, but this is only one-third of the land in need of consolidation. In some areas, the small and fragmented farms, which nowadays could not possibly yield a full-time livelihood, have become part-time holdings. This is especially true in South Germany, in Baden-Württemberg and parts of Bavaria, where the fragmentation is particularly bad, but where there is fortunately a widespread distribution of light industry in the many small towns. The farm family continue to live in the old village farmstead, but the farm is run by the wife, and frequently the grandmother, with the husband and perhaps the son helping in the evenings and at weekends. As long as the family is prepared to undertake the work involved, there is a very satisfactory solution to the problem. Moreover, once consolidation is achieved, amalgamation becomes possible, and is in fact taking place.

There is today a far more business-like attitude to agricultural policy than in the past. It is accepted that there will have to be a further movement of population out of the industry and more consolidation of farms. The aim of government policy is to bring about this transformation as painlessly as possible. The dilemma is that – from the purely economic point of view – the movement out of agriculture should be proceeding faster. But from a social point of view the movement is probably as fast as is tolerable or desirable.

READING

Hermann Höcherl, *Die Welt zwischen Hunger und Überfluss* (Seewald Verlag, 1969).

Graham Hallett, 'The Problem of Agriculture in a European Union', in *Journal of Agricultural Economics*, xx (1969) 3.

S. v. Frauendorfer and H. Haushofer, *Ideengeschichte der Agrarwirtschaft und Agrarpolitik*, 2 vols (B.L.V.-Verlagsgesellschaft, Munich).

John Marsh and Christopher Ritson, *Agricultural Policy and the Common Market* (Chatham House/PEP European Series No. 16, 1971).

5 The Communications Media

The Press

The first thing to realise about the West German press is that the Germans are not great newspaper readers, and in particular, not great readers of national newspapers. Most papers are regional and local. They are largely concerned with local affairs, but they also include news and editorials on national and international questions; the papers serving the big centres of population – such as Hamburg, the Ruhr or Stuttgart – are of a high standard. Thus the circulations given in table 32 are very small by comparison with those of the British popular papers. (However the readership per copy is high, because many cafés provide papers for their patrons.)

The only papers which are national, in the sense that *The Times* or the *Mirror* is national, are the *Frankfurter Allgemeine Zeitung*, *Die Welt* and *Bild-Zeitung*; the *Süddeutsche Zeitung* can also be considered national, although it has strong connections with Bavaria. The *Frankfurter* and *Welt* are 'qualities', *Bild* is a 'popular'. The 'best' paper – in the sense of having the best news coverage and the most informed comment – is undoubtedly the *Frankfurter*. The format is astonishingly dull – no pictures on the front page and not many elsewhere – and it rarely makes light reading, but its integrity, and the high quality of its articles, are seldom rivalled in any country. *Die Welt*, started by the publisher Axel Springer as a 'quality' companion to *Bild*, is more attractive in layout, and sometimes more readable, but it has less information and more tendentious comment than the *Frankfurter*.

The only paper with a circulation of millions is *Bild Zeitung*, the epitome of the popular paper or *Boulevard-Blatt*. This type of paper has been a relative newcomer to the German scene, for Germany had no such papers right up to the Second World War. German newspapers were either local, or solid and worthy, or organs of a political movement. (After 1933 all papers were, of course, strictly controlled, and only one political

Table 32

CIRCULATION OF NATIONAL NEWSPAPERS
AND THE MAIN REGIONAL NEWSPAPERS
(Average sales 1971, thousands)

National Papers

*Die Welt	218
*Welt am Sonntag	341
Frankfurter Allgemeine Zeitung	255
Süddeutsche Zeitung	264
Handelsblatt	60

Major Regional Papers

Westdeutsche Allgemeine Zeitung	561
Rheinische Post	342
*Hamburger Abendblatt	282
Neue Rhein-Zeitung	250
Ruhr-Nachrichten	232
Kölner Stadt-Anzeiger	219
Münchner Merkur	164
Frankfurter Rundschau	147
Koln. Rundschau	161
Stuttgarter Zeitung	156
Frankfurter Neue Presse	128
Bayernkurier	123

(*Berlin*)

Berliner Zeitung	319
*Morgenpost	201
Tagesspiegel	96

Illustrated Papers (weekly)

Stern	1583
Bunte Illustrierte	1677
Neue Revue	1564
Quick	1372
Jasmin	1055
Pardon	187
Konkret	142

'*Popular*' *Dailies*

*Bild-Zeitung	3393
Espress	335
Hamburger Morgenpost	267
Abendpost	125

'*Serious*' *Weeklies*

Spiegel	906
Die Zeit	290
Capital	165
Deutsche Zeitung/Christ und Welt	153
Rheinischer Merkur	51

* Springer group.

viewpoint permitted.) Under the Allied Occupation, a young publisher, Axel Springer, thought that there was a market for a cheap, short, popular paper which ordinary people – who certainly would not feel like tackling the *Frankfurter* – could read in the tram on the way to work. The format – lots of eye-catching headlines with very brief stories, with the usual quota of pin-ups and scandal – proved extremely successful, and was the foundation of the Springer publishing empire. But although it met a need at the time, it is hard to be very complimentary about *Bild*, which lacks the occasional well-written article, or the eloquent cartoons which distinguish the British popular papers.

Sunday papers are not as popular as in the United Kingdom, virtually the only ones being the Sunday companions of *Bild* and *Welt*. There are however weekly papers which have the same function as serious weekend reading. (Papers are very rarely delivered in Germany, but are bought at kiosks.) Probably the most distinguished weekly is *Die Zeit*, a voluminous paper of high quality, if inclined to literary obscurity. Its philosophy is 'liberal' in the traditional sense of tolerance, parliamentary democracy etc. although sometimes of the weak, self-doubting kind which is so conscious of how far Western countries fall short of the ideal that it fails to see much difference between America and Russia. A different type of weekly, with a larger circulation than all the other weeklies and 'Sundays' together, is *Der Spiegel*. This illustrated paper was originally a copy of *Time* – compact format with black and white photos on glossy paper. Its considerable bulk is made up of short articles on current news – usually of an 'exposé' type – with one very long article or extract from a forthcoming book. The style (*Spiegel-sprache*) resembles the breathless *Time*-style, with the use of ugly 'ieren'-words, even when adequate ones already exist – 'attackieren' instead of 'angreifen' etc. Like the Springer papers, it was originally the brainchild of one man – Rudolph Augstein – who is still the owner, although his sole editorship has recently been transformed into a collective editorship by a large number of journalists. The *Spiegel* very quickly achieved a large circulation because of readable muckraking, in the best sense of the term. It was not always as careful with its stories as it might have been, but when it devoted considerable effort to investigating a subject, it could produce real scoops. And although it always worked on the principle that good news is no news, it was, till the late 1960s, fairly catholic in its iconoclasm.

A typical case – a very revealing one from many points of view – is that of Herr Nurimand. Behman Nurimand was a Persian living in West Germany, who in 1967 published a book which, for a time created a stir.[1] The author professed to be a University lecturer in Iran, who had been dismissed for his political views. With what seemed to be a mass of empirical evidence, he painted an appalling picture of the state of the Iranian economy, and sought to show that the so-called 'land reform' instituted by the Shah was a fraud. The book not only attacked the Shah's rule but also sought to show how Iran, like all other poor countries, was exploited by 'capitalism'. Herr Nurimand became a cult figure among German undergraduates, and provided the intellectual basis for the demonstration against the state visit of the Shah to West Germany in 1968 which culminated in bomb attacks on the offices of the Springer group, and street riots.

The *Spiegel* investigated Herr Nurimand and his book in detail, sending reporters out to Iran. It produced a devastating article (*Spiegel*, no. 44, 1967) showing that his alleged academic career was pure fiction, and that the book was a mass of gross misrepresentations and errors, which could not possibly have been made in good faith. No one today denies that the book's attitude to facts was very casual. This had of course been clear to experts from the beginning, but it was the *Spiegel* which burst Herr Nurimand's popular reputation.[2]

In the last few years the amount of opinion, as distinct from fact, in the *Spiegel* has increased, and has become more pronouncedly 'New Left'. The general effect is often like reading *Neues Deutschland*. It would certainly be inconceivable today for the *Spiegel* to publish an article so damaging to the spokes-

[1] Behman Nurimand, *Persien, Modell eines Entwicklungslandes oder die Diktatur der Freien Welt* (Rowohlt, 1967).

[2] There was a sequel, also revealing. A translation of Herr Nurimand's book was published in the U.K. in 1969. *Iran – The New Imperialism in Action* (Monthly Review Press). The reviewer in *New Society*, who obviously knew nothing about the Spiegel article, accepted it as a valid account of conditions in Iran, which were likely to produce imminent revolution (24 July, 1969).

For a serious account of the Iranian land reform see Ann Lambton, *The Persian Land Reform 1962–66* (O.U.P., 1969).

men or doctrines of the Left as the Nurimand article. The headlines which accompany the often clever photomantages on the front page follow the same pattern: '*Ende des Wirtschafts-wunders*' (the slight recession of 1966/7), '*Faschismus in America*' (the trial of Angela Davies, not referring to the woman who wrote 'Let us bathe our hands in pigs' blood'), '*Staatsbankrott*' (the Schiller resignation).

Another group of periodicals which are at least quantitatively important are the illustrated weeklies, a type of paper, like *Paris Match*, with no parallel in the United Kingdom. As distinct from *Spiegel*, the *Illustrierten* are full of large colour photographs and the text tends to be 'popular'. However there are considerable differences between the papers. *Bunte Illustrierte* consists largely of travel articles. The others, at least, tend to be treated disparagingly by intellectuals. However *Stern* – and to a slightly lesser extent *Quick* – contain articles on social and political affairs, often of a surprisingly high standard. (And there is little point in producing a paper which is admirable but so dull that no one reads it; the author must confess that his regular newspaper reading when in Germany is *Frankfurter*, *Spiegel* and *Stern*.) Of the others, *Neue Illustrierte* is a '*Po- und Busenblatt*' and *Jasmin* is aimed at the female market.

At an even lower technical and intellectual level is the 'coloured press'. These are weeklies containing colour photos printed on ordinary newspaper, gossip and novelettes and – perhaps their most useful contribution – discreetly expressed but unambiguous 'contact' advertisements.

There is a wide range of papers with smaller circulations, including economic journals such as *Handelsblatt*, and papers representing a particular party or ideology. The latter includes *Vorwärts*, representing the Social Democrats; the *National-Zeitung*, which it is not unfair to describe as neo-Nazi; and various weeklies which combine sexual 'frankness' with radical-left politics (*Pardon, Konkret*).

Assessment

What assessment can one make of the West German press? This depends on one's political philosophy. To the critics of the New Left, all 'capitalist' publications are engaged in a conspiracy to deceive the public; the only hope lies in a non-commercial news medium which will be unbiased. (How a monopolistic, or state-supported newspaper industry might be expected to behave in practice, given the extensive experience with such systems in many countries, is rarely asked.) The following extract from a speech by a rising Young Socialist official, Herr Norbert Gansel, at the S.P.D. conference in May 1970 is typical of this increasingly influential view:

> Eine wirtschaftliche und politische Oligarchie hat sich in den ausschliesslichen Besitz der neuen Massenmedien gesetzt, die durch den technischen und technologischen Fortschritt eröffnet worden sind. Die Massenmedien dienen nicht der Kommunikation, sondern der einseitigen Durchsetzung von Macht-und Profitinteressen. . . . Leser, Hörer, Zuschauer sind als blosse Empfänger der Manipulation durch die unkontrollierte Botschaft hilflos ausgesetzt.

To explain the views of the *Kulturkritiker* to the press, the other organs of West German society, a brief diversion into Marxist theory is necessary. Marx had forecast that under capitalism the condition of the workers would get steadily worse, until they rose in violent revolution. But this did not happen, and the Russian revolution occurred in a primitive, rural country, where according to Marx, it could not happen. An explanation frequently given between the Wars was that, to forestall the workers' revolt, the capitalists would introduce a fascist dictatorship, using their control of the communications media to this end.[1] On this view, fascism – taking the form of National Socialism in Germany – was the last stage of capitalism.

This popular neo-Marxist theory of the 1930s – which can now be seen in historical perspective – is open to many objections. National Socialism enjoyed wide support among all classes, and the economic policies adopted by the National Socialists – such as price and rent freezes – were by no means in the interests of the 'capitalists' The allegedly 'fascist' communications media underwent a drastic change in 1933. Fascism

---

[1] Hermann Heller, *Staatslehre* (Leiden, 1934). An English equivalent is Harold Laski, *Parliamentary Government in England* (1938).

was not introduced in other countries, and was overthrown in Germany; and so on. The whole Heller-Laski argument looks rather foolish in the light of history, and in the 1950s was widely considered to have been discredited. In the late 1960s however many young German intellectuals – taking up the ideas of Herbert Marcuse in the United States and Jean-Paul Sartre in France – put forward very similar views, arguing that the seemingly liberal systems of West Germany, France, the United States and the United Kingdom were in fact already, or incipiently fascist.

Neo-marxist critics of *Spätkapitalismus* – who frequently write in the *Spiegel* – lose no opportunity to show how biased the 'bourgeois' press is. One article, available in English, which quotes their criticisms with qualified approval, criticises the *Frankfurter* for giving one-sided support to the revaluation of the Deutschmark, while criticising other papers for one-sidedly opposing it![1]

On the other hand, someone who rejects the neo-Marxist viewpoint, and believes that truth is best served by a clash of opinions, will not expect every newspaper article – least of all every article in a daily paper – to be as balanced and judicious as a historian writing several years later. For him, the question is whether the press provides for a range of viewpoints, with editors aiming to be accurate on matters of demonstrable fact. Some commentators who share this attitude, and by no means ally themselves with the neo-marxists, have criticised the 'monopoly position' and editorial policy of the Springer press. It is clear that the Springer papers do have a large circulation. However, because of the pattern of German newspaper reading, some of the figures quoted (for example ninety per cent of Sunday newspapers) are misleading. For both weeklies and dailies, several papers of differing shades of opinion are available throughout the Federal Republic. The only field in which the Springer press can be said to have a monopoly is in popular national dailies, where there is at present no competitor to *Bild*. This situation is the result of Herr Springer's commercial

---

[1] J. P. Payne, 'The German Press' in *Germany Today*, ed. J. P. Payne (Methuen, 1971), pp. 69–70.

See also Urs Jaeggi, *Macht und Herrschaft in der Bundesrepublik* (Fischer, 1969), p. 195 ff.

acumen in seeing the demand for a popular paper, and he has never sought to restrict competition. Indeed, the *Spiegel* was for a long time printed on the Springer presses!

As regards editorial 'slanting', it is certainly true that Herr Springer has used his papers to put forward his personal political philosophy – rather like Lord Beaverbrook (but unlike Lord Thomson). This philosophy has been outlined as follows: 'The Axel Springer publications stand for progress but oppose all attempts to destroy or subvert our society; support all peaceful moves to restore German unity in freedom; work for reconciliation between the Jewish and German people; reject any kind of political extremism; uphold the liberal market economy.' (Advertisement in *The Times*, 14 June 1969.)

The Springer press has, in recent years, criticised the *Ostpolitik* of the Brandt government, the Mao-ist-anarchist student movement, and the 'dirigiste' economic measures which led to the retirement of Professor Schiller. These are all reasonable views which deserve a hearing. They are sometimes put forward in a crude way which probably reduces their effectiveness, but a very strong case indeed can be made for the argument that, so long as the Russians are determined to retain their control of Eastern Europe, vague agreements like the Brandt treaties do no good, and may do some harm; that many of the New Left groups advocate a totalitarianism which would spell the end of the liberal West German system; that the recent moves away from a socially responsible market economy are politically as well as economically regrettable. It can hardly be said that there is now any shortage of opposing views. And the Springer press – unlike some of its strongest critics – has never advocated violence or unconstitutional methods.

Those who accuse the Springer press of actually distorting news often quote the case of the report in *Bild* that students in West Berlin had planned a bomb attack on Vice-President Humphrey in 1967, when as it turned out, the 'attack' was to be with flour bombs.[1] This may have been a deliberate misrepresentation, but it sounds rather like the sort of slip which can happen to any newspaper under the pressure of daily publication. To put it at the very lowest, there is no comparison with the systematic use of falsehood which has been practised

[1] Payne, *Germany Today*, p. 78.

when all news media are controlled by a party purportedly representing the people. In an open society, where there are not only other papers but also television and the foreign press, demonstrable lies cannot have a very long life. Nor is there any comparison with the vicious character assassination, the political hysteria and the calls for a violent overthrow of 'the system' found, on the one hand in the *National-Zeitung* and on the other, in the various underground or commercial publications of the Left.

All this does not mean that the Springer press is particularly admirable. One could wish for more 'Fairness' (the English word, interestingly enough, is used as there is no German equivalent) and a higher literary quality. It would also be a good thing if there were a differently-orientated (and better) competitor to *Bild*. But for an increasing number of people, the 'popular daily' is the television, so that even here talk of a *Meinungsmonopol* is somewhat exaggerated. In West Germany, as elsewhere, the future for newspapers probably lies with the detailed news and reflective comment which seem better suited to the printed word than the television screen. That is to say, the future probably lies with the 'qualities', and here the West German reader has a wider choice, among both daily and weekly papers than he has had in any previous era of German history. (There may have been more papers in the past, but they were local ones. In this field, as in industry, arguments that monopoly is increasing, which are based on total numbers of newspapers, or firms, can be misleading.)

Considering that the West German national press is largely a postwar creation, it has produced some very good papers, and is more vigorous and economically viable than might have been expected. It has some imbalances arising from the late development of a national press – such as only one popular daily – but the extent and danger of the 'Springer monopoly' has probably been exaggerated. Moreover, as has happened elsewhere in West German industry, and in newspapers in other countries, the personal rule of first-generation entrepreneurs like Herr Springer and Herr Augstein is being replaced by collective management. The West German press faces the problems of newspapers everywhere; combining good journalism with commercial success; rising costs and the competition of television;

the problem of who is to decide policy. But because most national papers are either quality dailies selling for a relatively high price (fifty Pfennig for the *Frankfurter*) or weeklies, the West German press has escaped the British problem of newspapers unable to make a profit with circulations of over a million.

There are changes that the author would like to see – more humour, a lighter touch and less preoccupation with internal affairs in the quality national dailies, a less tendentiously one-sided approach in the Springer and Augstein publications. But on the whole the West German press stands up well to international comparison, and deserves a better press than it often receives.

Broadcasting

The television habit developed later in the Federal Republic than in the United Kingdom, and is still a noticeably less pervasive element in the normal family's life. However the number of television sets has increased sharply in recent years, so that the number of sets per 1000 population is only slightly less than in the United Kingdom. Like radio, television in the Federal Republic is organised on 'public service' lines and financed mainly by licence fees. There was originally one public corporation, with a strong regional structure, but this monopoly was criticised, especially by the Social Democrats, who accused it of favouring the Christian Democrats. A second channel has been initiated, but is a public corporation and not, as in the United Kingdom, financed by advertising. A small amount of advertising is permitted, but it is concentrated in a single period of a quarter of an hour or so in the early evening, which at least avoids 'commercial breaks'. A third, 'cultural' channel has recently been started. There appears to be slight differences in the political colouring of the three channels, a common assessment being that '1' is Christian Democrat, '2' Social Democrat and '3' far Left. In general, West German television and radio is sober and didactic; its failings, if any, are more on the side of dullness than of triviality, in spite of a fair proportion of lightweight serials – some of them 'dubbed' versions of British or American products such as 'The Avengers' or 'Startrek'.

The organisation adopted for broadcasting – as compared

with the press – illustrates the limits on the commercial principle which the Federal Republic has imposed on its 'social market economy'. Commercial television never had much support, and although this was partly the result of the long German tradition of public service industries, there are good arguments for distinguishing between the press and television, even from a standpoint basically in favour of a market economy. Newspapers can be sold directly to the consumer, and competition is possible, since there are no technical barriers to starting new papers. In practice there is 'workable' competition in the

Table 33. TELEVISION SETS IN USE IN 1971.

	000	*per 000 population*
West Germany	15,970	262
France	10,121	201
United Kingdom	15,792	284

Source: E.E.C. Commission *Basic Statistics*, 1972.

German press in spite of its oligopolistic structure. Broadcasting on the other hand is a natural monopoly. Relying on sponsorship by companies, as in America, has well-known disadvantages, and even the British I.T.V. system involves 'commercial breaks'. A state-controlled system runs the danger of becoming an organ of the government, but the West Germans were very conscious of this danger after their experiences with the Nazis and instituted public corporations on 'B.B.C.' lines.

Comparing the West German communications industry as a whole with that in France and the United Kingdom, one can say that West Germany – in line with its federalistic history – has a more substantial range of regional and local papers than either of the other two countries. It has a small, but varied range of 'quality' national papers. With the not altogether happy exception of *Bild*, it has no popular national dailies on British lines, but a range of popular weeklies serves a similar purpose. West German broadcasting is more independent of the government than Radio-Television-Française, being more comparable to the British system, although more 'Reithian' than much current British broadcasting.

READING

Horst Holzer, 'Massenkommunikation und Demokratie in der Bundesrepublik Deutschland', in *Deutsche Gesellschaft im Wandel*, ed. K. M. Bolte (Opladen: Verlag Leske, 1970) Band 2.

Christian Longolius, *Fernsehen in Deutschland; Gesellschaftspolitische Aufgaben und Wirkungen eines Mediums* (Mainz: v. Hase und Kohler-Verlag, 1967).

Hans Dieter Müller, *Der Springer-Konzern. Eine kritische Studie* (Munich: Verlag Piper, 1968).

Hans Dieter Jaene, *Der Spiegel: Ein deutsches Nachrichtenmagazin* (Frankfurt: Fischer-Bücherei, 1968).

6 Controlling the Economy

Economic policy in the Federal Republic has been dominated by two long-serving Economics Ministers – Professor Ludwig Erhard (Economics Minister 1949–63) and Professor Karl Schiller (Economics Minister 1965–72). Both were economists turned politician, whose political careers ended unhappily, and both believed in a market economy rather than a centrally controlled economy, but they differed as much in their characters as in their contributions to economic policy. Erhard was a Bavarian member of the C.D.U., a man of transparent honesty, more a preacher than an intellectual, with a verbose and rambling style. Schiller was an S.P.D. member from Hamburg, tough, ambitious and hardworking, with a keen mind and an incisive style. Erhard had one big idea – that a market economy would work better than a centrally planned economy – and was able to affect the course of German history by implementing this idea at a time when it was by no means generally accepted. Schiller built on this foundation by introducing more sophisticated techniques, particularly in the fields of (a) short-term anti-cyclical measures (b) medium-term budgetary planning. A brief outline of the development of economic thought on these issues is necessary to explain the policies adopted in the Federal Republic.

Anti-cyclical Policies

The booms and slumps of the inter-war period, which caused massive unemployment, brought Hitler to power, and led to an upsurge of economic nationalism, caused more attention to be given to the problems of macro-economics, i.e. the factors determining the level of economic activity, rather than the problem of allocating resources between different uses. (The word *Konjunktur* expresses the idea of the level of economic activity better than any English expression and the somewhat unhappy translation 'conjuncture' has recently been coming into use.) The outcome was the development of 'Keynesian' ideas for combating depression by stimulating effective demand. In the event, the problems of the postwar era have been those of inflation rather than of depression. Admittedly, the Keynesian approach can be applied to booms as well as to slumps – by reducing demand rather than stimulating it. However the problem of 'creeping' cost inflation – deriving primarily from the bargaining power of trade unions in conditions of full employment – has proved singularly intractable even, in recent years, in West Germany.

The problem of *Konjunkturpolitik* is, briefly, to achieve the 'magic triangle' of full employment, stable prices and equilibrium in the balance of payments. (The aim of 'economic growth' is often added, as in the title of the 1967 'Law for the promotion of Economic Stability and Economic Growth'; but in fact economic growth has never been something that West Germany has been short of.) The level of unemployment can be influenced by altering the level of aggregate demand through budgetary or monetary policy. But postwar experience has shown that actions to boost or damp down the economy must be taken early in the trade cycle. If they are left till late in the short, shallow cycles which have characterised the postwar era, reflationary policies become effective only when the economy is already turning up, and deflationary policies when it is already turning down. Quite a good case can be made for the unorthodox view of Professor Milton Friedman that, given the inevitable time-lags in decision-making, 'fine tuning' is impossible, so that it is better to base budgetary policies on long-term trends.[1]

The second objective of the 'magic triangle' – a stable price level – has been the most difficult to achieve. Prices can be influenced (other things being equal!) by the level of employment and activity, since a condition of over-full employment will encourage prices to rise more than a condition of high unemployment. However experience has shown that, given strong trade unions, wages and prices can be forced up even when unemployment is at a level generally considered unacceptable.

[1] 'A Monetary and Fiscal Framework for Economic Stability', in *American Economic Review* (1948), p. 245. Reprinted in *Readings in Monetary Theory*, p. 369.

The third aim – equilibrium in the balance of payments – should be the easiest to achieve. The balance of payments is affected in the short term by the level of activity in the economy, and in the longer term by competitiveness and the exchange rate. The Bretton Woods agreement on postwar international financial arrangements envisaged that a country would move its exchange rate up or down if there were a 'fundamental disequilibrium' (i.e. a persistent tendency to surplus or deficit) in the balance of payments. Unfortunately most countries have, until recently, been slow to make such changes, whether downward or – as in the case of West Germany – upward.

Medium-term Economic Planning

The anti-cyclical policies mentioned above are very short-term. Should the economy be planned over a longer term? The early proponents of a 'social market economy' rejected 'planning', both the whole-hog type undertaken by the Nazis and Communists, which implied central control of all economic affairs, and the indicative planning practised in France.

Professor A. Müller-Armack – who coined the phrase *Soziale Marktwirtschaft* – opposes 'planning' on the ground that the responsibility for determining production levels must remain with the industrialist.

A free market economy rests upon the plans of individuals, who may plan for the short term . . . or some time ahead. Large firms must make fairly long-term plans for their capital projects, and, in my opinion, there is nothing against the Government, too, formulating its short-term budgetary policy at longer term with regard to certain fields such as transport and building . . . [but] forecasts, especially those relating to individual fields, are not bound to be fulfilled, so that in the event of the anticipated figures not being reached, [it must be ensured that] any measures taken do not paralyse the market.[1]

He remarks rather drily that the statistics necessary for making forecasts are not noticeably worse for Germany than for the 'planning' countries (France and the United Kingdom).

[1] 'The Principles of the Social Market Economy', in *The German Economic Review*, no. 2, vol. 3 (1963), p. 102. (An important article, unfortunately badly translated.)

But he adds that, in an economy experiencing dynamic change, it is not enough merely to rely on competition. The businessman inevitably tends to think in terms of short-run or medium-run profitability, and it is necessary for the state to initiate certain structural changes and moderate the impact of others.

This 'anti-planning' view therefore opposes attempts to control the output of particular industries, but it is not opposed to the government making longer-term budgetary plans – for as long ahead as it is possible to forecast – provided they are subject to revision. When the government budget takes a large proportion of the national income – as it does in West Germany – and when investments in roads, schools, hospitals etc. are planned several years ahead, it makes no sense to decide expenditure and taxation merely on a purely yearly basis. Plans for future expenditure need to be looked at in aggregate, to see how they compare with projected tax yields. In a reasonably fully-employed economy, and in the longer run Mr Micawber's advice on income and expenditure holds true for governments as well as individuals. The outcome was the 'medium-term financial planning' introduced by Professor Schiller.

Keynesian Economics

The view that government economic policy should be designed to achieve economic stability derives from the 'Keynesian revolution' in economics between the wars. The work of Lord Keynes and others led to a better understanding of some important economic problems (even if new problems have arisen to which economics has no answer!).[1] The new ideas gained rapid acceptance in the English-speaking countries, but were slower to be accepted in Germany, because of the stultifying effect of totalitarian control on intellectual life. In the 1920s, German economics was of a high standard, and excellent work was done by the *Institut für Konjunkturforschung* in Berlin, but the institute was closed by the Nazis, and many members left Germany. There was thus a 'missing generation' of economists after the war.

---

[1] There has also been a 'monetarist counter-revolution' which has reasserted the more traditional view that there is a connection between inflation and the money supply. The outcome however is tending to be a synthesis rather than the rejection of the Keynesian approach.

The outsome was that, in the early days of the Federal Republic prevalent ideas on the control of economic activity were distinctly pre-Keynesian. The economists of the Freiburg School accepted that it was the responsibility of the state to prevent deflation and inflation, but tended to think that this could be ensured by monetary policy alone; they had little concept of using budgetary policy to this end. In political circles, the prevailing view was that surpluses could be regarded in the same way as an individual's bank balance – that the positive balance resulting from a surplus could later be 'drawn upon' for current expenditure, irrespective of the state of employment. There was little understanding of the relationship between the flow of expenditure and of goods in the economy and the role that the state – if it is able to judge the macro-economic situation correctly – can play in maintaining a balance between the two. This is shown by the case of the 'Juliusturm'.

The 'Julius tower' was a Berlin fortress in which treasure obtained from France after the Franco-Prussian War had been stored, and the term came to have the figurative meaning of the state's accumulated reserves. During the period 1954/7 the Federal Government ran a budget surplus, and was thought to have built up a 'Juliusturm' which could be drawn upon to pay for increased state expenditure without raising taxation. The view economists would now take is that this reference to previous surpluses was meaningless. The current deficit would have been justifiable if there were unemployed resources in the economy, but what had happened in the past was irrelevant. However it is a sobering thought for economists that the Federal Republic, which started out with rather primitive ideas on economic policy, nevertheless managed on the whole to run her economy very well. In recent years the understanding of economic policy has improved, but at the same time – although this juxtaposition is no doubt unfair – the performance of the West German economy has declined somewhat!

A significant step in the introduction of a more sophisticated economic policy was the setting up in 1963 of an expert committee to review the economic situation and make recommendations (*Sachverständigenrat zur Begutachtung der gesamtwirtschaftlichen Entwicklung*). The committee consists of five professors, and their reports contain both excellent surveys of the current economic situation and recommendations which, whether or not they are accepted, have had a considerable effect in educating informed opinion on economic matters.

'Konjuktur' in West Germany

Economic problems in West Germany have gone through several phases. The initial postwar problem was one of suppressed inflation, followed by 'frictional' unemployment. After the 'economic miracle', there was a boom in the early 1960s, arising from governmental over-spending (or under-taxing) in the run-up to an election. This was followed by a short recession in 1966/7; at this time, new instruments for controlling the economy were introduced. The recession was followed by an unsteady recovery, accompanied by growing inflation. During this period West Germany ran persistent balance of payments surpluses; however at the end of 1972, the fundamental disequilibrium seemed to have been corrected by successive revaluations. In 1972, the wheel seemed to have come full circle, with a pre-election boom!

The 'economic miracle' began with the currency reform of June 1948. In the previous years the economy had fallen into a state of chaos, which was not so much the result of the war devastation and the inflow of refugees as of a breakdown in the monetary system. The suppressed inflation of the Hitler period had resulted in the accumulation of large liquid funds, which were isolated from the economic system by an elaborate system of controls. Only German thoroughness enabled this control system to work at all, and after capitulation it began to break down. The effect of people trying to spend their cash balances would normally have been to cause a large rise in prices, but the official prices of many essential goods were still pegged at or near their prewar level. The result was that large quantities of goods disappeared into the black market, where they fetched prices many times their controlled level. The production of goods at controlled prices became unprofitable, and the bizarre situation arose that, at a time when people were severely short of food and clothing, the production of ash trays and cigarette lighters boomed, since they were not subject to price control. As the gap between controlled prices and black market prices widened, people began to lose confidence in money and to revert to barter. They made long journeys on foot or by bicycle into the country to exchange their possessions with farmers for potatoes or milk. Walter Eucken was indisputably correct when he wrote at the time that both the centrally planned economy and the price mechanism had collapsed. 'The failure of money and the central administration of the economy has led to increasing self-sufficiency of economic units and to the emergence of a system of barter, two things incompatible with an extensive division of labour. The economic system is reduced to a primitive condition.'[1]

The Currency Reform

It became clear that a drastic reduction in the money stock was essential if economic recovery was to begin, and this was eventually carried out in June 1948. Every adult was given 60 units of a new currency, the Deutschmark (about £5) and holdings of the old currency, Reichmarks, were later exchanged for Deutschmarks in the ratio of 100 to 6·5. The results were sudden and startling. The shops, which had been empty, filled with goods, and industrial production, which had stagnated in the previous years, began a sudden upsurge, rising by 50% within the year. It has often been argued since that time that the economic 'miracle' was not really miraculous, but merely the outcome of a gifted and industrious people rebuilding their shattered economy. This is true, but the startling change between the period before and after July 1948 indicates the extent to which an economic system can either frustrate individual efforts or give them the opportunity to be effective.

The currency reform as such was supported and prepared by the Allied authorities, but they did not favour the relaxation of controls which was carried out at the same time; this was largely due to the insistence of Dr Ludwig Erhard and strongly criticised by the British and American authorities, as well as the Social Democrats. But this bonfire of controls worked very much better than had been expected, just as it did in Great Britain in the 1950s.

Although the results of the currency reform were in general so beneficial, an unpleasant new factor soon began to develop – unemployment. Previously there had been tremendous disguised

[1] *The Foundations of Economics*, p. 226

unemployment but little actual unemployment. Large numbers of people had taken very unproductive jobs on farms, mainly in return for their keep, while in other occupations the fixed wages meant so little in terms of purchasing power that workers were taken on out of charity, even when there was virtually nothing for them to do. After the currency reform, when money again had some value, unemployment grew and reached a peak of 10·2% in 1950. As to the causes of this unemployment, a difference of opinion arose between the German and Allied Authorities. The Allied Authorities, accepting the view of some British economists, argued that it was due to insufficient de-mand, and advocated a more relaxed monetary and budgetary policy together with more physical controls.[1] The German Authorities argued that the unemployment was frictional and transitional, caused by the continuing inflow of refugees, who had difficulty in immediately finding work, especially as many of them had settled in the Lander alongside the border, Schleswig-Holstein, Lower Saxony, Hessen and Bavaria, which were relatively poor in industry. They therefore argued that a 'reflationary' policy would merely cause inflation, and that unemployment would disappear as industry got into its stride. As things turned out, the German Authorities had on the whole the better of the argument, although the Korean boom probably came at a fortunate time. Unemployment fell steadily from 1950 onwards and was running at under 1% from 1961–6 (table 34).

[1] 'Dr Erhard, the Minister of Economic Affairs and his satellite economists nevertheless seem to regard this development [the increase in production] as a conclusive vindication of their attitude to social and economic problems and of the "liberalist" policy pursued. Nothing could be further from the case. Unemployment has remained substantially above the dismal figure of 1949. The level of production is still at least 15 % below the level which could be attained in the short run by *appropriate planning and control*.' T. Balogh, *Germany: An Example of 'Planning' by the 'Free' Price Mechanism* (Oxford, 1950), p. 67.

Lord Balogh expressed a common British view when he wrote of 'an iniquitous new German economic and social system' and of a 'repetition of the 1930s' (p. 72). He also made the following forecast which, unlike much of what economists write, can be proved right or wrong. 'Much productive effort, especially investment, is misdirected by luxury demand into hotels, restaurants, cinemas, shops and the industries that serve them. . . . In the long run this income pattern will become intolerable and this productive pattern unsafe. . . . When the attempt is made to recreate mass demand and to wrench the production system into another shape, a serious crisis and terrible social costs will be inevitable' (p. 6).

Table 34

UNEMPLOYMENT

	Workers on Short-time (000)	Unemployed Nos. (000)	%	Unfilled Vacancies (000)
1952	79	1385	6·1	129
1956	25	765	3·1	236
1960	1	270	1·3	539
1962	2	154	0·7	607
1964	—	169	0·8	671
1966	6	161	0·7	536
1967	44	459	2·1	336
1968	—	323	1·5	609
1969	1	178	0·9	833
1970	7	148	0·7	811
1971	60	185	0·9	648
1972 May	81	208	1·0	576

Source: *Monatsberichte der deutschen Bundesbank.*

Economic Growth without Inflation

In the 1950s it looked as though West Germany had discovered the secret of full employment and economic growth without inflation. The rise in prices during this period was among the lowest in developed countries, comparable with that in the United States, and very much less than in Great Britain or France. Retail prices rose by 20% in the decade 1950–60 compared with 50% in Great Britain. But in the 1960s prices rose more sharply.

Part of the explanation was that, in the early 1950s unemployment and the competition of refugees on the labour market helped to moderate wage increases – although wages still increased very sharply. Even after full employment had been reached, the trade unions exercised moderation in wage claims, while at the same time output went on rising much faster than anyone had thought possible. The combined effect was a low rise in labour costs per unit of output, and hence a low rate of price increases. After about 1960, the trade unions came to regard annual increases in real wages of up to 8% as normal and began to be more ambitious in their claims. But at the same time the rate of growth of the economy began to slow down.

This flattening off of the growth curve was only to be expected; the phenomenal growth rates of the 1950s were to some extent the result of 'catching-up' after the effects of the war, and of the tremendous movement of labour out of agriculture. Nevertheless the fall to a normal growth rate, just at the time when people had begun to become accustomed to abnormal ones, caused the rate of price increase to jump sharply.

Table 35

YEARLY PERCENTAGE CHANGES IN PRODUCTIVITY, WAGES AND PRICES

Productivity (G.N.P. per head at constant prices)		*Gross Wages and Salaries per Employee*	*Retail Prices*
1950–61 average	+ 7·0	+ 8·0	+ 1·3
1961	+ 4·2	+ 10·2	+ 2·3
1962	+ 3·3	+ 9·0	+ 3·0
1963	+ 3·0	+ 6·1	+ 3·0
1964	+ 6·3	+ 8·9	+ 2·3
1965	+ 4·9	+ 9·0	+ 3·4
1966	+ 3·1	+ 7·2	+ 3·5
1967	+ 2·8	+ 3·2	+ 1·4
1968	+ 6·8	+ 6·1	+ 1·5
1969	+ 6·1	+ 9·2	+ 2·8
1970	+ 3·5	+ 14·7	+ 3·7
1971	+ 2·6	+ 11·9	+ 5·2
1972 (1st quarter)		+ 9·3	+ 5·5

Source: *20 Jahre Leistung in Zahlen 1970; Monatsberichte der Bundesbank.*

This pressure on prices from the cost side was aggravated by pressure from the demand side. In the 1950s, the government had pursued a fairly disinflationary budgetary policy. But public expenditure rose faster than taxation receipts in the years 1963–6, and mainly for this reason the economy became by any standards overheated. The too inflationary budgetary policy of these years was the result partly of weaknesses in the economic organisation of the Federal Republic, partly of failings in the Erhard administration. The organisational weakness was that, before 1967 it was very difficult to use taxation as an anti-cyclical measure. In particular, it was impossible to use changes in Income and Corporation Tax for this purpose. Since the receipts from these taxes were divided in a fixed proportion between the Federal and the *Länder* Governments, any change in tax rates involved protracted discussions between the various governments. In consequence, tax changes, when finally agreed upon, tended to be introduced at an unfortunate time, from the point of view of counter-cyclical policy. Thus in the early 1960s, it was felt that the sharply rising level of income was raising tax receipts unnecessarily; discussions on a reduction in tax rates lasted several years and the change was finally made in 1964, at a time when the economy was showing distinct signs of overheating.

Boom and Recession

When the boom began to get out of hand in 1965, the Erhard Government was to some extent limited in its armoury of fiscal powers, but it did not make full use of those powers it had. The constitution of the Federal Republic does not contain the useful House of Commons rule that only the Government can propose measures involving financial expenditure, but it does allow the Chancellor to veto any proposals passed by the Bundestag. In the spring of 1965, in a mood of pre-election generosity, Christian Democrat members of the Bundestag passed a row of economic and social measures involving substantially increased expenditure, which, in the absence of tax increases, were bound to have inflationary consequences. Dr Erhard deplored this reckless expenditure but did not use his powers as Chancellor to stop it. In this, as in other ways, Dr Erhard, who had been an outstanding Economics Minister, proved an ineffective Chancellor.

The inflationary developments in 1965 convinced many Germans that a stronger armoury of counter-cyclical powers was needed, and the outcome was the Economic Stabilisation Bill presented to the Bundestag in the summer of 1966. This bill laid down that the budget was to be used for counter-cyclical policies, although it tackled the problem solely from the side of expenditure and investment. It empowered the Federal Government to make long-term budgets which were to be revised each year, and to lay similar obligations on the *Länder*. It empowered the Federal Government, for limited periods in times of boom, to restrict access to the capital market by *Länder* Governments and local authorities, to reduce depreciation allowances in these circumstances.

The Economic Stabilisation Bill introduced by the Erhard Government was designed to cope with inflation, but it was clear even before it was introduced that the boom had passed its peak, and was turning into a slump. In early 1966 the Bundesbank sought to combat the inflationary situation by means of harsh credit restrictions. These deflationary measures were too late and too severe, and accelerated the downturn into recession. The number of unemployed rose from around 140,000 at the beginning of 1966 to over 600,000 in the summer of 1967, while during the same period the number of unfilled places fell from 600,000 to 300,000. The unemployment would have been higher if the immigrant workers had not absorbed some of the unemployment. These workers – unlike their Commonwealth counterparts in Britain – normally have a year's contract and, except in the case of the Italians, no right of permanent residence, unless they have qualified for German citizenship. In 1966 their contracts were often not renewed and their total members fell from 1·3 million at the beginning of the year to 991,000 in September 1967. Thus the recession, although short-lived, was by postwar standards quite sharp; in the first six months of 1967 the Gross National fell by 2 % compared with the corresponding period of 1965.

The recession was a shock to the euphoria that had been developing in the 1960s, and was greeted in much of the Press with exaggerated lamentations. Some of the older economic journalists, who had always felt that there was something unseemly in the steadily growing prosperity of the Federal Republic, took pleasure in saying 'I told you it couldn't last'. However the recession, although it indicated the need for more precise short-term management of the economy, and some shift of emphasis in longer-term policy, was not really a reflection of any deep-rooted malaise. It was only the down-swing in the type of business cycle which has become almost classic in the postwar period: over-full employment and inflation, followed by deflationary measures at a time when the boom is already passed its peak, leading to a sharp down-turn and moderate under-employment.

The Grand Coalition

When the 'Grand Coalition' of Christian Democrats and Social Democrats came to power in November 1966, the Ministry of Economic Affairs was taken over by a professional economist, Professor Karl Schiller, of a distinct 'Keynesian' type. Professor Schiller believed in a market economy, but also in the need for state intervention to maintain full employment while curbing inflation. He sought to put across his economic ideas by coining a spate of expressions of the type to which the German language lends itself – *globale Steuerung* (global guidance, i.e. manipulation of economic aggregate and is investment or consumption without interfering in the actions of individual firms) or *Konzertierte Aktion* (concerted action, i.e. co-operation, although of a somewhat vague character, between groups such as trade unions, employers and the government). He contrasted his 'enlightened market economy' with Erhard's 'naive market economy' and announced 'We give pride of place to the statistic rather than the sermon.' (Later however he spoke with respect of Erhard's achievements.)

It was clear when the 'grand coalition' came to power that the economy was running well below capacity, and among economists there was fairly general support for reflationary policies. In their report at the end of 1966 the 'five wise men' of the *Sachverständigenrat* called for a 'controlled expansion', and this view was strongly shared by Professor Schiller. The process of reflation was however complicated by both legalistic and by longer-term considerations. The recession had brought about a fall in tax receipts, and hence a budget deficit. This was in itself a 'built-in stabiliser', which should not have given rise to concern. However the constitution of the Federal Republic – drawn up in the light of pre-Keynesian ideas – required that the Federal budget be balanced, and there were some circles in government and industry who thought that a budget deficit necessarily meant inflation. There were also some longer-term considerations. It was already clear before the recession that there was a downward trend in the rate of increase of G.N.P. At the same time some items of government expenditure showed a rising long-term trend – for example, pensions, as a result of automatically adjusted pensions and a rising proportion of retired persons in the population. In the longer term therefore there was a case for some increase in taxes.

The steps by the Kiesinger Government in the spring of 1967 to deal with the depression consisted mainly of measures designed to stimulate investment – an increase in public investment by both the Federal Government and the *Länder* Governments and an increased depreciation allowance for private firms. The increased public expenditure was contained in a 'supplementary budget' which was a device to preserve the appearance that the main budget was balanced. There was also provision for a 3% increase in income tax rates for incomes over £1600 per annum. This increase in taxation was regarded as inappropriate by most British commentators (the *Spectator* headed a leading article 'The Irresponsible Germans'). However the increase was to become effective only on 1 January 1968, when recovery expected to be under way, as indeed proved to be the case. The net reflationary effect of the measure taken by the Kiesinger Government were, as it turned out, adequate; at that stage in the cycle, a greater measure of reflation would have led to over-heating of the economy later in 1968.

By the end of 1967 it was clear that the *Talsohle* (valley bottom) of the recession had been passed, and that recovery was on the way. Between May and October 1967, the number of unemployed fell from 629,000 to 341,000, and all the economic indicators began to turn up. In its monthly report for October 1967, the *Bundesbank* noted the symptoms of an incipient cyclical upswing, although they were not yet very strong. Several reports issued by economic institutes toward the end of 1967 foresaw a recovery in 1968, although the detailed forecasts varied. By the middle of 1968 expansion was well under way, with a growth rate of 5%.

During the recession, exports rose sharply, and the balanced payments surplus rose to a record level. A fall in home demand obviously leads German firms to switch quickly to exports. The German authorities however managed to prevent this trade surplus from causing a rise in German reserves – and a fall in deficit countries' reserves – by lending funds abroad in various ways. Thus some of the criticism of West Germany for pursuing 'bad creditor' policies in 1967 was unjustified. However, this was only a short-term remedy. Over the period 1963–7 Germany was in 'basic disequilibrium' because of its tendency to a balance of payments surplus.

The Economic Stabilisation Act

In addition to moderately reflationary policies for dealing with the current recession, the Kiesinger Government provided itself in 1967 with the economic armoury for a long-term counter-cyclical policy. It took over the 'Economic Stabilisation Bill' from the Erhard Government and extended its provision considerably. Whereas the old Bill was primarily framed to combat booms, the new one was designed to ensure steady growth avoiding both booms and slumps. It added to the first Bill the provisions that, in any year, 7% of investment can be freed from Income and Corporation Tax, if the government desires to stimulate investment, and that Income Tax and Corporation Tax can be raised or lowered by up to 10% in any year. It also laid down that, when economic stability is endangered, the federal government should lay down 'economic guidelines' (*Orientierungsdaten*) for the guidance of public bodies.

The recession brought about a change in the general German attitude to inflation and deflation. Up till 1967 German thinking was strongly influenced by the memory of the runaway inflation of 1922, which ruined large numbers of middle-class people, and of the suppressed inflation before the 1948 currency reform. Inflation was regarded as the great evil, and the dangers of recession not rated highly. Subsequently, the dangers of recession have been rated higher, and the dangers of inflation lower.

Recovery and Inflation

The period from 1969 to 1972 was one of uneven recovery, characterised by higher rates of inflation than before. Boom conditions developed in 1969 and 1970, with profits rising, unemployment falling below 1%, and the number of unfilled vacancies once again far exceeding the number of unemployed. In 1970 workers became more militant in pursuing wage claims and using strike action if they were not met. Wage claims of 12–15% were submitted, and often conceded by employers as being less harmful to them than a strike. One argument for large wage claims – and in many quarters a criticism of the whole capitalist system – was the sharp upturn in company profits in 1968. The downturn in 1966–7 was overlooked (Table 18, p. 28).

Professor Schiller – following his policy of early intervention in the trade cycle – responded to the overheating in 1970 with a 10% surcharge on income tax and corporation tax. This levy was made possible by the Economic Stabilisation Act. The legislation embodying the levy laid down that it was to be repaid by 1973, when it was expected that the economy would have turned down (a nice theory, like Lord Keynes's scheme for postwar credits, which didn't quite work out). There was also a revaluation of the Deutschmark by some 8% in 1969. This probably overdue move was primarily undertaken to reduce the large trading surpluses which Germany had been earning since the recession, but it also came at a convenient time to damp down the home market by increasing the supply of goods. Attempts were also made to get down the level of wage claims both by persuasion (*konzertierte Aktion*) and by encouraging industry to stand up to strikes. In December 1971 there was a three-week strike by the metal-workers over a two-figure claim which was eventually settled for 7·5%. This heralded a decrease in wage claims, although they still remained at inflationary levels.

But these anti-inflationary measures seemed for a time to be tending to cause the economy to turn down again. Orders levelled off in 1970, and this was followed by a cutting down of industrial development. But this incipient recession did not materialise: in 1972 orders picked up, and real G.N.P. started to rise at around 3%. Moreover, unemployment did not rise as much in 1971 as might have been expected from the trends in productivity and output. Firms had learned from the experience of 1967/8. At that time, firms had dismissed workers as soon as orders fell off. This harmed industrial relations; moreover, within a year the firms had to scramble to re-engage workers. In 1971 firms relied on short-time working wherever possible – a socially far better arrangement for a *temporary* decline in orders.

External Problems

Between 1969 and 1972 there were several changes in the exchange value of the Deutschmark, resulting in a substantial rise in relation to other major currencies (table 36). The effect, combined with the upward trend of German prices, was to restore an approximate equilibrium in the current balance of

Table 36

EXCHANGE RATES

No. of D.M. equal to one:	*Franc*	*Pound*	*U.S. Dollar*
1966	·81	11·17	4·00
1968	·81	9·58	3·99
Dec 1971	·66	8·78	3·66
May 9 1973	·62	7·10	2·84

Source: *Statistisches Jahrbuch* and financial press.

payments. The balance on goods levelled out at around D.M. 15 billion, while the deficit on services and remittances rose steadily with the expansion of the economy (table 37). In 1972 the Deutschmark seemed to be correctly valued as far as trade and long-term capital movements were concerned.

Table 37

BALANCE OF PAYMENTS
(million D.M.)

	Current A/c			*Capital A/c*	*Change in Reserves*
	Total	*Goods*	*Services*	*Remittances*		
1961	+ 2·8	+ 6·6	+ 0·1	− 4·4	− 4·3	− 2·3
1962	− 1·9	+ 3·5	− 0·2	− 5·2	− 0·2	− 0·9
1963	+ 0·7	+ 6·0	− 0·3	− 5·1	+ 2·3	+ 2·7
1964	0	+ 6·1	− 0·8	− 5·3	− 1·7	+ 0·4
1965	− 6·7	+ 1·2	− 1·6	− 6·4	+ 2·4	− 1·3
1966	0	+ 7·9	− 1·6	− 6·3	+ 0·9	+ 1·9
1967	+ 9·4	+ 16·8	− 1·0	− 6·4	− 10·0	− 0·1
1968	+ 10·9	+ 18·3	− 0·1	− 7·3	− 7·3	+ 7·0
1969	+ 6·2	+ 15·5	− 0·9	− 8·4	− 19·0	− 14·4
1970	+ 2·7	+ 15·7	− 3·9	− 9·0	+ 11·0	+ 22·6
1971	+ 0·4	+ 15·9	− 4·9	− 10·5	+ 7·4	+ 10·9
1972*	+ 0·2	+ 4·5	− 1·1	− 3·2	− 2·6	+ 3·9

Source: *Monatsberichte der Bundesbank.*

* 1st quarter.

However, the exchange rate changes and international financial crises of the period 1970–2 caused the Deutschmark to be subject to speculative pressures. When holders of other currencies believed that a declaration of that currency was imminent, they tended to move into Deutschmarks, to protect the value of their holdings. (These 'speculators' are primarily large trading companies rather than 'gnomes'.) This inflow of 'hot' money was disturbing, and tended to have inflationary consequences. Thus the German authorities found themselves in a dilemma. In principle they favoured the free international movement of capital. The Nazis had operated strict exchange control, and Ludwig Erhard once described it as the 'symbol of evil'. There had been almost complete freedom of capital movements since the early 1950s – in marked contrast to France or Britain. At the end of 1971 however the government decided that measures were necessary to stop the inflow of speculative capital. At first an attempt was made to deal with the problem without resorting to direct controls. An order was introduced which compelled persons transferring money to Germany to leave a proportion on deposit with the *Bundesbank*, free of interest (*Bardepot*). This was in effect a form of tax, and was defended by Professor Schiller as being a *'marktkonfom'* measure. But there was strong pressure from the Bundesbank to introduce direct controls. In June 1972 the Cabinet decided – against the opposition of Professor Schiller – to introduce controls on the purchase by foreigners of German securities. Professor Schiller – arguing that this control would inevitably lead to others – resigned in protest.

Professor Schiller's Resignation

This issue was however merely the last straw for Professor Schiller, who had been becoming steadily more isolated from the Cabinet and the leaders of the S.P.D. In this alienation, Professor Schiller's own abrasive character, and lack of political feel, played a role. There was something a little naive in his comment after the last Cabinet meeting 'I was amazed that my proposals were not accepted, in spite of my good arguments'. Yet there were deep issues of principle in the growing dispute between the leaders of the S.P.D. and the man who had been one of the party's main draws with the general public. During

the period of the S.P.D.–F.D.P. coalition, the S.P.D. moved
markedly to the Left. The Young Socialists, in effect, rejected
the Godesberg Programme and returned to the policy of
complete state ownership of the means of production, distribution and exchange which had been the party's policy in the
immediate postwar years. Without going so far, many leading
members of the party became sceptical of 'social market
economy' and 'global guidance'; they began to favour a more
dirigiste economic policy. They also began to diverge from
Professor Schiller in their attitude to inflation. The view gained
wide acceptance that, so long as its victims were compensated
(for example through 'dynamic pensions') an annual inflation
of 4, 5 or 6% was nothing to worry about, and certainly unimportant compared with other objectives, such as the fullest
possible level of employment. This view was unacceptable to
Professor Schiller who, although he was unable to prevent
inflation, remained convinced that the maintenance of the value
of money was essential to a free society. His departure thus
symbolises a change in the German attitude to inflation. (His
successor, Mr Helmut Schmidt, coined the slogan, 'Better 5%
inflation than 5% unemployment'.)

Professor Schiller also differed from his colleagues on
budgetary questions, as he made clear in his letter of resignation.
(This was officially private, but it was clearly written for
publication since everything is eventually leaked in Bonn.) The
latter was published by *Quick*. It is well worth reading, and is
available in a rather clumsy translation in *The Times* of 11
August 1972.

Professor Schiller pointed out that on forecasts for the next
few years, planned expenditure was tending to outrun revenue.
It was necessary either to increase taxation or to cut planned
expenditure. However the government – after the battles over
the Eastern treaties with a tiny majority – had agreed to premature elections in the autumn of 1972, and the more profes-
sionally political members of the Cabinet obviously thought
that the Finance Minister was out of his mind in talking about
raising taxes and reducing expenditure at such a time. As the
letter puts it with shrewd under-statement.

The memorable meeting of May 16, 1972, when the Minister in charge of Finance found himself exposed to undisciplined attacks just because he pointed to the additional burden indicated by the medium-term financial planning, should just be mentioned. . . . And still the Cabinet refuses, in the summer of 1972, to occupy itself with the facts that determine financial planning from 1973 on . . . I am not prepared to support a policy which to the public conveys the impression that the Government lived with the motto 'After us the deluge'.

The resignation of Professor Schiller was widely regarded as having a more than personal significance. Dr Erhard saw it as heralding a general attack on the free market economy. Although he had obviously been hurt by Schiller's earlier disparaging references to him, and had hit back, he now recognised that Schiller had continued and developed the tradition he founded (*Die Welt*, 7 July 1972). Müller-Armack also took the view that the Social Democrats had, in effect, torn up the Godesberg programme. But other economists – not of a Marxist persuasion – argue that in many fields more state control is inevitable and desirable.

Whatever view one takes of his more general philosophy, Professor Schiller showed excellent judgement in the more technical management of the economy. He was right in judging the reflationary measures needed in 1967/8 and the deflationary measures needed in 1970. He correctly judged the amount of Deutschmark revaluation needed, and he will almost certainly be shown to have been right in his views on medium-term budgetary policy. His technical competence won wide approval in German industry.

Many of Professor Schiller's forebodings were soon realised. In February 1973, the Government announced a series of tax rises. These included a 'temporary' 10 per cent surcharge for three years on Corporation Tax and Income Tax on high incomes, a rise in petrol tax, and reductions in investment allowances. Perhaps the most striking feature of the measures was the explicit acceptance of a 6 per cent inflation rate.

Shortly afterwards the West German economic institutes, in one of their periodic reports on the economy, were unanimous on the need for further action to control demand inflation – although not on the methods to be employed. In May the annual rate of inflation had risen to 8 per cent, and the government introduced further anti-inflationary measures – rises in taxation and a tax on investment. It was all very much the sort of intervention under the pressure of events, late in the cycle, against which Professor Schiller had so often warned. On the international side, the physical controls on capital movements had become more and more extensive.

The economic situation in early 1973 was therefore mixed. There was full employment, rising productivity, and equilibrium on the current balance of payments. But the rate of inflation was high and accelerating, while the issues of *Konjunkturpolitik* which had been avoided in the run-up to the election were coming home to roost. The SPD, having seemingly rejected the clear-cut liberal philosophy of Professor Schiller without accepting the totalitarianism of the Young Socialists, was tending towards an *ad hoc* interventionism with little regard for long-term consequences. It is a type of situation previously more characteristic of the U.K. than of the Federal Republic. Although its economy remains basically very healthy, West Germany has acquired more than a few symptoms of the 'English sickness".

READING

Ludwig Erhard, *Wohlstand für Alle* (1957) translated as *Prosperity through Competition* (London, 1958).

Herbert Giersch, *Growth, Cycles and Exchange Rates – The Experience of West Germany* (Stockholm: Almquist and Wiksell, 1970).

— *Kontroverse Fragen der Wirtschaftspolitik* (Munich: Piper, 1971).

Karl Uhl, *Aspekte der Wirtschaftspolitik* (Frankfurt: Verlag Moritz Diesterweg, 1968).

Jahreswirtschaftsberichte der Bundesregierung (Bonn: Verlag Dr Hans Heger).

Sachverständigenrat zur Begutachtung gesamtwirtschaftlicher Entwicklung: Jahresgutachten (Bonn: Verlag Dr Hans Heger).

7 Industrial Relations and Social Security

A foreigner who spends any length of time in a country is bound to form impressions of the way social relations work. These impressions – which will say just as much about his own country – are probably as important as anything he reads in sociological studies. The author – as an Englishman in West Germany – was struck by the clearly defined distinctions of status, combined with a relative absence of class distinctions. That is to say, there are clearly defined chains of command in government and industry, and people are conscious of their status in the organisation, as shown by the use of functional titles as a form of address – 'Herr Direktor', 'Herr Regierungsrat' – or even (a nice and useful touch) 'Herr Ober', short for 'Herr Oberkellner', for waiters. At the same time there is considerable uniformity of life-style. German directors and trade unionists dress and look alike, their homes are furnished in the same sort of style, with differing degrees of lavishness, and they speak alike. There are strong regional accents, but hardly any class accents. (Coming back to South-East England, one could scarcely believe that people were not putting on caricatures of upper-class and lower-class accents.) Similarly, the owner of a German factory, for example, will usually live in the town where it is situated and will be in his office at 8.30, or earlier, every morning. There has never been the British tradition of living as a country gentleman once you had made money in industry (which may partly explain why British agriculture is more efficient than German, but British industry less efficient, and British towns more squalid).

The consciousness of status, or rank, mentioned above, does not imply attitudes of subservience or arrogance. There is plenty of give-and-take and indeed less feeling of 'them and us' than in Britain. One had the impression that in German industrial firms, workers can take grievances to management and have them listened to, while managers take the trouble to explain new policies in good time, and obtain workers' co-operation. Can these impressions be explained by the development of German social institutions?

Some illumination can be obtained from the most readable of German sociologists, who poses the question of how Nazism was possible, and how social conditions in the Federal Republic differ from those of the pre-Nazi era.[1] He points out that the industrial middle class which grew up during Germany's industrialisation under the Bismarckian Empire was subservient, in political and social outlook, to the army officers, landowners and higher civil servants who ruled Prussia and the Empire. They never clashed with this ruling class, as the rising British classes who were 'in trade' had clashed with the landowners earlier in the nineteenth century. Thus many of the characteristics of German society before 1933 – the authoritarian structure of the family, the paternalist-military organisation of industry, the lack of liberalism in political and social thought – were the result of the unchallenged dominance of a class more characteristic of a pre-industrial society. Thus German capitalism was subordinated to the state, and lacked the political and social dynamism which characterised it elsewhere (but also, one might add, the ruthless commercialism and the neglect of the poor). The traditions of central control and obedience to the state continued, even when the state was taken over by demagogic barbarians.

Under the Federal Republic, events took a different course.

In contrast to the first industrialisation, the industrial recovery after 1945 was carried out by industrial firms themselves. In spite of all the restrictions by the state which are inevitable in the middle of the twentieth century, the state did not feel that it had a responsibility to control and direct industrial corporations. . . .[2]

The result has been that the upper class in the Federal Republic has risen out of industry, and is no longer subservient to any

[1] R. Dahrendorf, 'Demokratie und Sozialstruktur in Deutschland' in *Gesellschaft und Freiheit* (Munich, 1963).
[2] Dahrendorf, in *Gesellschaft und Freiheit*, p. 297 (author's translation).

higher class. The result has been an increased emphasis on the personal pursuit of success, an economic and political pluralism, and a weakening of authoritarian attitudes, as seen in the 'citizen in uniform' army, or the equality insisted on by German wives. Professor Dahrendorf adds that one cannot guarantee the stability of the new system, and that it is open to attack by 'utopian' ideologies (as, indeed with the neo-Marxist student movement, has now happened).

This analysis of Professor Dahrendorf may not be the whole story, but it is convincing. The Federal Republic has taken over some institutions and mannerisms which date from the Empire, but have filled them with a completely different spirit. In West Germany the whole feel of society has become much more 'American'.

Sociological writings like those of Professor Dahrendorf provide a useful background, but to understand current controversies, one needs to look at particular social institutions in more detail. In this chapter I shall review briefly the systems of industrial relations and social security.

Industrial Relations

After 1945, the West German trade unions, which had been disbanded in 1933, were reorganised under allied prompting. Before 1933, they had been weakened by being frequently divided into Roman Catholic and secular unions. They were reorganised into sixteen unions, primarily on an industrial basis, so that a car firm, for example, will negotiate simply with the Metalworkers Union, instead of the twenty-odd in the British car industry. The unions are grouped together in a federation, the *Deutscher Gewerkschaftsbund* (D.G.B.) which is very active in campaigning on various issues, such as *Mitbestimmung*. German trade unions levy quite substantial fees, pay sufficient salaries to attract men of calibre and are on the whole impressive organisations – somewhat like the more reputable American unions. However, they represent only a minority of German workers, the proportion of employees belonging to unions of the D.G.B. is thirty per cent, and has remained at roughly this level since 1950.

In the immediate postwar years, some trade union leaders sought to make the trade unions into militant anti-capitalist organisations, using their power to bring about a fully state-owned economy. But, just as the S.P.D. changed its policy in the 'Godesberg Programme', so the trade unions, in the 1950s, came to accept the 'social market economy', and a role as one interest group in it. More recently there have been signs of a swing back to the attitudes of the late 1940s. The President of the D.G.B., Herr Vetter, has described the Federal Republic as a 'class society' and is therefore opposed to trade unions sitting down with employers under Professor Schiller's 'concerted action'. Similarly there have been calls for price control and nationalisation.

The German unions have invested their funds in various commercial enterprises, and are today big employers. They are sole owners of *Neue Heimat*, the largest building concern in Europe, and have majority holdings in the *Bank für Gemein-wirtschaft*, the fourth largest national bank, in the *Volksfürsorge*, the largest insurance company, as well as in the third largest building society (*Bausparkasse*) and the largest food wholesaler.

Believers in a 'social market economy' support this participation in the market by trade unions. It increases competition, gives trade unions practical knowledge of management problems, and helps to make the market economy more acceptable by showing that the participants are not merely hard-faced tycoons. Conversely, opponents of the market economy are opposed to trade unions giving it any respectability by participating. The neo-Marxist movement, which is so influential in the Universities and dominates the junior branch of the S.P.D., is strongly opposed to trade unions 'supporting capitalism' by, for example, building houses through *Neue Heimat*. They believe that all trade union funds should be reserved for political and industrial action to 'overthrow capitalism' – a return in a more violent form to the ideas of the late 1940s.

Although the organisation of German trade unions, and their contribution to, for example, solving the housing problem, is something which other countries might well study, the German system of industrial relations is even more interesting. Relations between employees and management have taken a different course in West Germany from that in Britain or France. In Britain, when it became clear that the ordinary civil law was unsuitable for industrial relations, they were excluded from legal control (Trades Disputes Act 1906) and developed outside it – until recently. In Germany, the principle was accepted in the nineteenth century that a special body of labour law was needed to guarantee certain rights to employees, in return for the acceptance of certain obligations.

Any such system of labour law must be based on a view of the status of employees in an enterprise. One view, which has a long history in Germany, urged that the employee should not merely be protected in matters such as hours of work and arbitrary dismissal, but should be given an active say in the running of the enterprise, at least on matters directly affecting him. Proposals for 'factory committees', including representatives of the workers, were included in the manifesto of the national assembly of 1848, but were not put into practice. The present system had its origin in 1918 when revolutionary committees of workers were set up in some factories. Although the revolution itself was suppressed, provision for works councils were included in the constitution of the Weimar Republic, and this tradition was taken up by the Federal Republic, mainly under the Works Constitution Law (*Betriebsverfassungsgesetz*) of 1952.

Workers' participation in the Federal Republic takes place at two distinct levels – the supervisory board and the works council. To explain representation on the supervisory board (*Mitbestimmung* or 'co-determination') it needs to be made clear that, under German law, public companies have *two* boards of directors – a supervisory board (*Aufsichtsrat*) which meets only three or four times a year, to examine financial results and broad policy, and a board of executive directors (*Vorstand*) which meets frequently and takes the important business decisions. The *Vorstand* is elected by the supervisory board. In a normal company, two-thirds of the supervisory board is elected by the shareholders; as banks and financial institutions are important shareholders, bankers figure prominently among the membership of supervisory boards. The remaining one-third is elected by the employees; two have to be employees, and the remainder are usually trade union officials. The employee-elected members receive the normal directors' salary and are bound by the normal rules in confidential matters. However, their presence means that the employees and the trade unions are represented in the appointment of the *Vorstand*, and in high-level decisions.

The arrangements for *Mitbestimmung* in the coal and steel industry (*Montanindustrie*) are somewhat different. After the war, the trade unions wanted these industries nationalised. As a second best, they obtained more employee representation. Half – instead of one-third – of the supervisory board is elected by the employees. Moreover, on the board of executive directors, one director (*Arbeitsdirektor*) is especially responsible for personnel questions, and the person appointed to this post has to have the approval of the employees; he cannot be appointed against their veto.

The second type of employee representation is at the level of the works (*Betrieb*) rather than the firm, and is thus referred to as the 'works constitution' (*Betriebsverfassung*). This is a far more down-to-earth affair, concerned with practical work-place problems, rather than the high-level issues discussed by the supervisory board. In each works with over five employees, a works council (*Betriebsrat*) has to be elected by the employees, which negotiates with the management. The works councils take no part in wage negotiations (apart from questions of detailed application); this is a matter for trade unions. Nor do they have competence in decisions on products, prices etc., which are reserved for the *Vorstand*. But in many of the detailed questions of working arrangements, which can cause so much resentment (and so many strikes in Britain) they have extensive rights, spelled out in detail in the 1952 and 1972 laws. Some matters have to be decided jointly by works council and management – mainly times of beginning and ending work, working conditions, methods of paying wages, new production methods etc. They must be consulted on questions of hiring and firing. They must be informed on the company's personnel plans and its financial situation, and have rights to examine company records. In firms with more than 100 employees, a further body has to be set up, the economic committee (*Wirtschaftsausschuss*). This is a small committee of four to eight members, of which half are nominated by the works council and half by the management. Its function is to discuss economic and technical prospects and future production programmes; the aim is to give employees a better understanding of what is happening, prepare them for future changes, and convey shop-floor feeling back to management.

The works council (and economic committee) has been an unqualified success. It is accepted as much by management as by employees, and the thorough discussion of work-place problems undoubtedly contributes to West Germany's relative freedom from strikes. The *Deutscher Gewerkschaftsbund* has however always had a slightly ambivalent attitude to the works councils, since they are elected by all employees – of whom only a quarter are members of trade unions. The D.G.B. has shown more interest in *Mitbestimmung*, and has campaigned strongly for an extension to all firms of the arrangement in the coal and steel industry, whereby the employees elect half the members of the supervisory board (*paritätische Mitbestimmung*). The employers federations are opposed to this change. The C.D.U. and F.D.U. have also tended to be against it, but in 1968 the Grand Coalition appointed the Biedenkopf commission to investigate the working of *Mitbestimmung* in the coal and steel industries and make recommendations. In the next year, before the commission had reported, the S.P.D. adopted the policy of *paritätische Mitbestimmung*. The argument by the trade unions and the S.P.D. is that labour plays as important a role in industry as capital, and should therefore have an equal voice in management. They argue that workers will only accept the authority of management if they feel that they have a share in it, and that social justice requires '*paritätische Mitbestimmung*'.

The arguments against it are partly on grounds of principle, partly practical. The present economic system is based on the principle that in the last resort the shareholders bear the risk and the responsibility for the management of companies. Under the proposed arrangements, shareholders would bear the risk but be deprived of the responsibility, which would put the system of private industry and the market economy in doubt. The employee representatives (often trade union officials, under the coal and steel arrangements) would represent both management and labour, and thus have a divided responsibility; how would they deal with inflationary wage demands, or a situation which – in the interests of consumers – required a reduction in the labour force? The arrangements would also, it is argued, lead to indecisiveness and delay in management. Finally, opponents of *'paritätische Mitbestimmung'* argue that the important thing for the worker is the speedy settlement of work-place grievances through the works councils. The fact that there is someone formally representing him 'up there' on the supervisory board means little or nothing to him.

What evidence is there on these questions? Surveys have shown that workers are indeed more conscious of the works council than of their representation on the supervisory board, but this is more an argument for the importance of the works council than against *paritätische Mitbestimmung*. There is also some evidence that *Mitbestimmung* has slowed down decision-making. As one American observer comments:

> The legally prescribed and enforceable distribution of equal parts of power among members of the Managing Board apparently even changes the character of decision making. The more or less pronounced domination of the Board by a *de jure* or *de facto* president that is standard in most German enterprises has been replaced by 'horsetrading' (*Kuhhandel*) between equals, with consequences of delay and non-functional argument. If no agreement can be reached immediately on controversial issues, they frequently are postponed.[1]

However, provided that eventual decision-making is not inhibited, it is no bad thing for employee and trade union viewpoints to be thoroughly thrashed over at the highest level.

The most detailed study of the subject is contained in the report of the Biedenkopf commission, which consisted of professors, assisted by representatives of trade unions and management. The commission came to the conclusion that the arrangements in the coal and steel industry could be cleared of some of the criticisms sometimes made. On the other hand they had certain disadvantages, they had not been outstandingly successful (as compared with arrangements in other industries) and should not be extended to other industries. The equal division in the supervisory board often led to the postponement

[1] Heinz Hartmann, *Authority and Organisation in German Management* (Princeton University Press, 1959), p. 69.

of decisions, while the ambivalent position of the *Arbeits-direktor* in the *Vorstand* was unsatisfactory. Management in the coal and steel industry did not take more account of social consequences than in other industries where it was already normal practice to do this. Thus the commission made various detailed proposals for electoral and organisational methods, but did not recommend *paritätische Mitbestimmung*.

This report had no effect on the advocacy by the D.G.B. and S.P.D. of '*paritätische Mitbestimmung*', but the S.P.D. had to shelve its implementation in order to obtain the support of the Free Democrats in the coalition government formed in 1969. If in the future the S.P.D. were able to form a government by itself, it might well introduce *paritätische Mitbestimmung*. What would be the outcome? Probably neither as beneficial as its advocates suggest, nor as catastrophic as its opponents suggest. As the Biedenkopf commission confirmed, the employee representatives are just as anxious as the shareholder representatives for the firm to make a profit. The fact that the existing arrangements – both in coal and steel, and elsewhere – have worked tolerably satisfactorily for twenty years indicates a basic community of interest, which is more important than representation percentages. On the other hand, the arguments of the trade unions that the dignity of man requires *paritätische Mitbestimmung* need to be viewed with some scepticism. What matters most for employees are the arrangements for speedily solving work-place problems. If the aim is to give 'countervailing power' to trade unions, *paritätische Mitbestimmung* may be a legitimate objective. If the aim is to improve life for the ordinary worker, then attention should probably be focused on the *Betriebsverfassung*.

Although negotiations at the works councils level settle many issues of working conditions, there is also an extensive body of labour law enforced by special Labour Courts which gives workers both rights and responsibilities. There is a considerable measure of job security. Minimum periods of notice ranging from two weeks to six months are laid down, with even more favourable provisions for long-service office workers. But an Act of 1951 on 'Protection against Dismissal' goes further, and limits the employer's right to dismiss any worker to cases where dismissal is 'socially justifiable'. Notice of large-scale dismissals has to be given to the Labour Exchange, together with the comments of the works council, and such dismissals can be carried out only after a prescribed interval. Moreover an individual worker can appeal against dismissal to the Labour Courts, and his dismissal cannot be sustained unless the employee can prove that the dismissal is justified either on personal or on pressing business grounds. In the event few cases go to court, but the existence of this provision helps to prevent arbitrary dismissal, or the threat of it. There are still stricter limitations on the right to dismiss disabled persons, members of works councils, or expectant mothers (who are entitled to six weeks off before confinement, and eight after, on full pay).

On the other side of the picture, the right to strike is also subject to legal controls. Strikes as such are legal, and unions cannot be sued for their consequences when the proper procedure is followed and the strike is not in breach of a contract between employers and unions. The procedure laid down

Table 38

NUMBERS OF WORKERS INVOLVED IN STRIKES
(000)

	1967	1968	1969	1970	1971
Germany (F.R.)	60	25	90	184	536
France	2804	464	1510	1160	3,234
United Kingdom		2258	1665	1801	1,178

Source: *Statistisches Jahrbuch*, Internationale Übersichten.

includes the holding of a strike ballot among members. If the procedure is not followed or if the strike is, like most British strikes, unofficial, it does not enjoy the protection of the law and employers can sue employees for financial losses caused by it. In practice, strikes are more often threatened than actually called, and the number of working days lost through strikes is much less than in most other industrial countries.

Social Security

Compulsory social insurance was introduced by Bismarck in 1881, and the German scheme was a model for many other countries. Although since modified enormously in detail, the basic organisational structure of the Bismarckian scheme has remained unaltered, even though it is in some ways no longer appropriate. Hence the growing discussion of the need to reform the system. In terms of total resources directed to social insurance however West Germany is very high in the international league table (18·2 per cent of G.N.P. in 1971). And although there are some striking exceptions, most people are well supported in old age, disability or sickness.

Unlike France or Britain, West Germany does not have a centralised scheme of old age and sickness insurance, but a large number of independent semi-official bodies. These are organised on local or industrial lines and have the legal form of a public corporation (*Gesellschaft des öffentlichen Rechtes*), with representatives of management and trade unions on the board. Except for old-age insurance, these organisations are self-financing, although subject to official supervision. Contributions are a percentage of income, and benefits depend on the contributions paid. There were originally separate schemes for wage-earners (*Arbeiter*) and salary-earners (*Angestellte*), although this distinction has tended to become blurred. There are separate arrangements for civil servants (*Beamte*) who include a wide range of occupations, such as school and university teachers.

Health insurance is undertaken by some 2000 separate health funds (*Krankenkassen*), financed by equal contributions from employees and employers. The percentage rates – up to a controlled maximum – can be fixed by the individual *Krankenkassen*, in the light of their expenses. The health funds make their own arrangements with doctors and hospitals, so that contributors receive treatment free. They do not have to pay first, and claim a refund later, as in France. They do however have to pay a proportion of the cost of drugs and dental treatment, and in hospitals it is usually only the basic service (third class) which is provided free. More individual attention, both medical and non-medical (private room, phone etc.) can be obtained by paying the extra cost.

One feature of the German medical scene which is in marked contrast to that in France or Britain is the popularity of the *Kur* (cure). This involves going to a resort with medicinal springs – or at least mountain air (*Luftkurort*) – and for three weeks or so, under mild medical supervision, taking the waters, going for walks, swimming or taking massage and saunas etc. Since they are also enjoined to exercise moderation in eating and drinking, the patients naturally go home feeling much refreshed. It may only be a kind of holiday, but it is very different from the common type of holiday which begins by driving from Hamburg to Italy, which (as the Germans, ever thorough, have shown by clinical tests) leaves the German husband more exhausted than when he started. Many of the *Krankenkassen* will, on a doctor's certificate that the patient is run down, pay for a *Kur*, and every year three million Germans take one at some eighty spas throughout the Federal Republic. They compensate for the strains of German business life, and keep a lot of people out of hospital; although the Germans do not work as hard as they used to, they still work pretty hard. (But although the *Kur* as a form of preventive medicine is something that other countries might well emulate, it cannot be regarded as an outcome of the prevailing system of social insurance, since the Russians take the waters at Black Sea resorts just as earnestly.) The spas have worked hard to provide modern facilities and avoid the fate of the British and French Edwardian spas. Many of them are excellent places to spend a holiday as they provide extensive sporting and recreational facilities (although the town council of Freudenstadt, a pleasant Black Forest spa, recently turned down the offer of a Swiss company to build a *Freudenhaus*).[1]

In recent years, the *Krankenkassen* have come under increasing financial pressures as a result of changes common to all developed countries: the rapid escalation of costs resulting from new methods of treatment, the increased readiness to call in the doctor, and the fact that people today survive in an

[1] For the most part, West Germany has adopted the policy of tolerating prostitution, provided it is carried out discreetly, or in specified districts. There are houses in all the big cities, run by private enterprise but subject to official supervision, as well as higher class call-girls. The German *Sexualhelferin* (to quote a recent survey by R. B. Alexander, *Die Prostitution in Deutschland*, Kindler, 1969) for the most part provides her services to the frustrated and lonely with decorum and in attractive accommodation. There is little of the exploitation and criminality which exists when prostitution is suppressed. In accordance with the general official policy, pornographic material may not be displayed, but straightforward 'business guides' may be sold to adults (*Der Strich*, Dülk Verlag, 1971).

invalid state who, until recently, would have died. Proposals have been made for a more uniform and egalitarian system. The D.G.B. has proposed the abolition of classes of medical treatment in hospitals, although it does not object to patients being able to buy extra non-medical facilities. Moreover the highly fragmented organisation of the health funds is almost certainly not one which would be chosen if a system were being instituted today. There are also criticisms of the relation of senior and junior doctors in hospitals, of a kind familiar to British ears. West Germany differs from Britain however in not having an extreme shortage of home-produced doctors, probably because they earn more.

The discussion on detailed questions of organisation has tended to divert attention from the fundamental dilemma – common to all affluent countries – that there is virtually no limit to the amount of money that can be absorbed by modern medicine – for 'intensive care' units to keep dying people alive at all costs, organ transplants etc. Limits have to be imposed, if not by patients' ability to pay, then by administrative decision. But a few lone voices question the basic approach of modern medicine. There was a strong 'health reform' movement in Germany earlier in the century, which contributed to the thriving state of German spas. There are still some people who argue that a great deal of surgery and drug treatment is only treating symptoms; that more emphasis should be placed on positive health, through natural diet and appropriate exercise; that incurably ill people should be allowed to die in peace. These views are still heretical, but more may be heard of them.

Pensions

As with health insurance there are various vocational pension funds, although far fewer in number. They were originally self-financing, with pensions depending on contributions. However, as a result of inflation and the desire to give old people a higher pension than they had paid for, the state has intervened to subsidise the pensions paid. In 1957, legislation was introduced whereby all pensions were to be raised annually in accordance with the average rise in earnings (*dynamische Renten*). This means that the pensions are not merely raised to compensate for the rise in prices, but are raised in line with the rise in the standard of living of current wage- and salary-earners. Pensions have in fact been raised each year since 1957 by from five to ten per cent. But although a substantial part of the pension comes from the state, the amount an individual receives depends on the contributions he has made. Thus although most people do in fact retire on half to two-thirds of their current income, the system is so complex that it is difficult to know in advance what one's pension will be, and some people qualify for relatively little.

The pension funds originally covered employees, and have gradually been extended to cover other groups, such as self-employed tradesmen and farmers. The coverage is now fairly comprehensive, although there are still some pensioners – mainly women – who because they have not qualified by contributions, receive only very small pensions. The distribution of pensions received under the compulsory scheme is given in table 39. (The British state pension for a single person in 1970 was D.M. 170.)

Table 39

PENSIONERS' NET INCOME FROM THE COMPULSORY SCHEME 1970

D.M. per month	Men	Women
	%	%
over 600 D.M.	46·6	15·3
300–600	43·5	55·8
150–300	8·4	24·0
under 150	1·5	4·9
	100·0	100·0

The problem of people on low pensions has recently received increasing attention. There is a widespread feeling that benefits should not depend as much as they do at present on the number of contributions paid.

There are two main issues concerning pensions: firstly the complexity of a system in which independent funds, based on the principle of benefits according to contributions, have been gradually underpinned by state subsidies; secondly the heavy and rising budgetary cost of 'dynamic pensions', at a time when the proportion of pensioners in the population is rising. There has been a good deal of discussion of these issues, but no clear policy has yet emerged.

In addition to the contributory pensions, there are extensive grants for people who become handicapped, or otherwise suffered in the war and, as a safety net under the health, old age, and unemployment insurance schemes, there is the system of 'social aid' (*soziale Hilfe*) for anyone who has fallen on hard times. For persons of working age, this has increasingly become a matter of financing retraining or rehabilitation, but for elderly people it can take the form of a cash payment, dependent on their level of income. Social aid is administered by government agencies.

The Social Budget

In the 1950s social security policies were largely *ad hoc*, and took little account of the total effect on the economy. But as expenditure rose it became clear that social security was a large item in both the government budget and the national income,

Table 40

SOCIAL BUDGET
(000 million D.M.)

	Pensions insurance	Health, accident and unemployment insurance	Various†	Pensions etc. for civil servants	War pensions and compensation payments	Total social budget
1960	18·4	12·4	3·0	7·9	5·0	46·7
1965	29·4	20·4	7·0	12·5	8·5	77·8
1968	40·2	28·0	7·9	14·9	9·1	100·1
1970	48·2	29·8	10·1	18·0	9·8	115·9
1973*	60·1	39·1	14·0	22·2	10·5	145·9

Source: *Survey of Social Security*, p. 26.

    * Forecast.

    † Children's allowances, Social Aid, Aid for Youth, Rent Allowances.

and that some assessment of trends in receipts and expenditure was necessary. Since 1968 a 'social budget' has been drawn up by the federal government. This is an extension of the 'medium-term economic forecasting' introduced by Professor Schiller; it involves assessing expenditure and contributions for five years ahead, assuming that current provisions are continued. The projections show expenditure rising as a percentage of national income, and indicate that benefits will have to be curbed or contributions raised (table 40). Professor Schiller's insistence on the unpalatable fact that expenditure in this field has to be financed was one of the causes of his alienation from his Cabinet colleagues, leading to his resignation in 1972.

Conclusions

In the fields of industrial relations and social security, the term 'social' in the Federal Republic's 'social market economy' is justified. West Germany has thus developed a unique system of industrial relations which has been extremely successful in dealing in a human way with the problems of industrial change. It has also devoted a high proportion of its growing wealth to helping the old and the sick, with some exceptions resulting from maintaining a system in which benefits depend on contributions. Although the systems of health and old-age insurance on the whole stand up well to international comparison, in their details they contain a lot of historical ballast, and will probably be extensively modified before long.

READING

Industrial Relations

See entries under 'Deutscher Gewerkschaftsbund', 'Mitbestimmung' and 'Betriebsverfassung' in *Staatslexikon* and *Handwörterbuch*.

Dr A. Klein 'Social Policy in Germany' and 'Federal Ministry of Labour and the Social Structure', in *Co-determination and the law governing Works Councils and Staff Representation in the Public Services* (1963).

Mitbestimmung – eine Forderung unserer Zeit (Düsseldorf: Deutscher Gewerkschaftsbund, 1971).

Mitbestimmung – Forderungen und Tatsachen (Köln: Deutsches Industrieinstitut, 1971).

Gisbert Kley, *Co-determination in coal and steel – Replies to the D.G.B.'s demands* (Köln: Bundesvereinigung der deutschen Arbeitgeberverbände).

Biedenkopf-Kommission, *Mitbestimmung im Unternehmen. Bericht der Sachverständigenkommission zur Auswertung der bisherigen Erfahrungen bei der Mitbestimmung* (Bonn: Verlag Dr Hans Heger, 1970).

H. A. Clegg, *A New Approach to Industrial Democracy* (Oxford: Blackwell, 1960).

Campbell Balfour, *Industrial Relations in the Common Market* (Routledge and Kegan Paul, 1972).

Social Insurance

Entries under 'Rentenversicherung' and 'Krankenversicherung' in *Staats-lexikon* and *Handwörterbuch*.

The Federal Minister for Labour and Social Affairs, *Survey of Social Security in the Federal Republic of Germany* (1970).

8 Education

Education plays an important role in any modern economy, from two points of view. (a) its general effect on economic and social life, and (b) its 'streaming' effect in training different categories of young people for various rungs on the economic and social ladder. It is fairly clear that when a large proportion of the population are educated – in the perhaps somewhat old-fashioned sense of being able to think and express views rationally, possessing a wide knowledge and the ability to acquire new knowledge – that population will be better able to cope with economic, social and political problems than one that is not so educated. However, the primarily quantitative approach to education which has become fashionable in the postwar era can produce unexpected social results. The intolerant and in-articulate undergraduate, capable only of shouting down those with whom he disagrees, was presumably not quite what the exponents of the expansion of higher education had in mind. There is now a tendency to question the type of 'economics of education', fashionable in the early 1960s, which assumed that public expenditure producing x per cent increase in university places, would lead to y per cent growth in national income, with – implicitly – only beneficial social effects.

In West Germany there has been considerable criticism that too little has been spent on education. In the last few years expenditure on all forms of education has risen sharply, and is likely to continue rising. Although this increased expenditure is almost certainly desirable, it may be doubted whether, by itself, it will achieve all the beneficial results that have been forecast. The second aspect of the education system – in particular the degree of equality of opportunity – has also received considerable attention from critics of the West German system. In an age in which 'qualifications' are all-important, the educational opportunities available to children can strongly influence the positions in life which they later occupy. It is claimed – with considerable justice – that the West German school system does little to compensate for the differences in family circumstances, and provides markedly different educational opportunities to different groups – the main differences being between town and country. More general criticisms are that there is too sharp a distinction between academic and practical training, and that the social, as distinct from the intellectual virtues are neglected. The special problems of the universities must be considered separately.

The School System[1]

In the nineteenth century, German education was world-renowned. The system of compulsory schooling, well-established by the middle of the century, was a model for the United Kingdom. The extensive German system of vocational training was also widely admired. In the two decades before the First World War, when Germany was rapidly overtaking Britain in the industrial field, many shrewd observers pointed out that the difference was not at the level of university graduates, but at the 'N.C.O. level' (literally in the German case). Thanks to her technical schools and institutes, Germany had far more salesmen and mechanics who were not only skilled in their trade but also had a wider education, and a foreign language.

This system – developed and freed from military connections under the Weimar Republic – has, in essentials, been recreated by the Federal Republic. The schools are predominantly state-run day schools. There are a few private boarding schools, and the right to set up private schools is guaranteed in the constitution, but (unlike British 'public schools') private schools in Germany are unimportant. School begins at six years of age; rather surprisingly *Kindergarten* are rare. Compulsory full-time schooling continues to fifteen and, for those who leave then, there is compulsory part-time attendance at trade schools until eighteen, in conjunction with apprenticeship (*Lehre*).

Education is the responsibility of the *Länder*, so that school arrangements differ from *Land* to *Land*. Some co-ordination is however achieved by a Standing Conference of Education Ministers. This diversity provides opportunities for experimentation on a regional basis. Critics of the federal system on the

[1] For a more detailed description, see Claessens, Klönne and Tschoepe, *Sozialkunde der Bundesrepublik* (Diederichs, 1965), p. 337 ff.

other hand maintain that federalism delays reforms, and that more central control is needed. The Social and Free Democrats subscribe to this view, although no steps in this direction were taken by the Brandt government. A further complication is the existence, in several *Länder*, of separate Catholic and Protestant schools (at the elementary *Volkschule* level). The denominational school results primarily from the demands of the Roman Catholics, since the Evangelical church is ready to accept secular schools (*Gemeindeschulen*) provided that religious education is supplied.

The basic school, which all children attend up to the age of ten, is the *Volkschule*. At ten there is the opportunity to leave for two other types of school, the *Gymnasium* and the *Realschule*. But at present some three-quarters of West German children remain in the *Volkschule* till they leave at fifteen. The *Gymnasium* is the equivalent of the English grammar school, in that it gives a straight academic education, which leads to university entry. It differs however (or has done until very recently) in the length, breadth and intensity of study. The matriculation certificate, the *Abitur* is taken at nineteen. Most students take seven or eight subjects, including both arts and sciences; there is not the early specialisation of the English system and the work load is, from the very beginning, extremely heavy.

Since about 1970 however this system has begun to be changed. Although some schools maintain the traditional standards, others have begun to adopt a much less rigorous programme; there is a move to allow a more limited choice of subjects in the *Abitur* and no longer to insist on 'precise' subjects such as mathematics and languages.

The *Realschule* (or *Mittelschule*) at which students remain to sixteen, gives a more practical, and less demanding education, designed for 'middling' positions in industry or the civil service. In addition there is a complex range of vocational institutes which provide technical or commercial training, mainly for students who have left the *Volkschule* or *Realschule*. These technical institutes however often provide good vocational training for holders of the *Abitur*, some of whom start at the university and drop out. The traditional German system is thus one of compulsory schooling at a fairly low level from six to fifteen, followed by part-time vocational training and apprenticeship, except for the minority who switch at ten to more advanced schools, which open the way to higher education. In recent years this system has come under increasing criticism.

Criticisms of the System

There is no doubt that the most unsatisfactory part of the German system is the *Volkschule* after the age of ten. Those who leave it at the age of fifteen – the majority of Germans – have received only a rudimentary education, even though they are assured of day-release training till eighteen. The position of the *Volkschule* is particularly bad in country districts, where facilities are poorest and where a number of one-class schools still exist. The problem is partly one of a shortage of teachers. At the end of the war, two-thirds of the teachers were missing, and although the numbers have increased, so have the number of students. Teachers in Germany are civil servants (*Beamte*) and in the past this meant security, a pension and some status. With greater opportunities in industry and elsewhere, together with the trend – not confined to Germany – for teachers to be held in less respect, the attractiveness of being a teacher has declined.

Students who merely attend the *Volkschule* do however receive part-time education, in conjunction with apprenticeships, up to the age of eighteen. At any one time, some one and a half million West Germans are attending such courses, and virtually everyone acquires some qualification, if only as a shop assistant or hairdresser. This comprehensive system has in the past been of great value, and is still, for example, an advance on the British system, in which youngsters can be thrown on the labour market at fifteen without any training at all. The results are apparent; anyone who shops in the two countries notices the difference in the competence of shop assistants. However the day release/apprenticeship system has come under criticism for instilling traditional skills, rather than the more flexible approach needed for changing modern technology. In the last few years there have been demonstrations by apprentices, complaining that the so-called apprenticeship is a waste of time ('*Lehrzeit ist Leerzeit*') largely spent making cups of coffee for the *Meister*. These criticisms have been combined with neo-Marxist attacks on Western society in general, and it is hard to know how far they are justified. Some firms have introduced excellent modern systems of theoretically based training, for example, apprentices are taught the general principles of metal-working before being introduced to the particular machines they will operate. However some of the criticisms are probably justified in many smaller firms.

A more general criticism of the whole educational system is that large sections of the population do not in practice have the opportunity to realise their potential, even though in theory all types of education are open to everyone. The relatively late age at which school begins – six – combined with the absence of nursery schools, means that home conditions have a marked effect on the child's progress. Many children from professional families can read when they come to school, and have a head-start. Hence the demand for nursery schools, to reduce intellectual and social differences arising from family background. At the age of ten, children in towns and children from middle-class parents receive more encouragement to move out to higher schools than children of working class parents, who are often quite happy to see their children leave school at the legal minimum and start their apprenticeship. These family influences, combined with the relative absence of grants for university study, mean that there is a lower proportion of children of working-class parents at universities than in the United Kingdom or France. One sociologist draws a striking comparison: 'There are about a million agricultural workers in the Federal Republic, and from these families precisely eighty University students enrolled in 1958. There are also about a million civil servants: from their families 52,199 students enrolled at the same time.'[1]

Professor Dahrendorf has also criticised the lack of a 'socialising' *ethos*, i.e. the emphasis is on learning, and there are relatively few sports and extra-curricular activities to develop public activities such as 'getting on with others', 'playing the game', etc. The effect is to produce the 'unpolitical' German, an insecure basis for democracy. By contrast, he holds

[1] R. Dahrendorf, *Arbeiterkinder in deutschen Universitäten* (Tübingen, 1965), p. 7.

up the English system as a model.[1] The criticism is a valid
one of many German and French schools, even though,
ironically, the English 'playing the game' syndrome, which
Dahrendorf so admired, already seems to belong to a vanishing
world.

Does the school system constitute a '*Deutsche Bildungs-
katastrophe*' (to quote the title of a book published in 1965)?[2]
Certainly the achievements of the Federal Republic are least
impressive in the field of education. Yet the German system
has its good points, and in some ways provides a sound basis
for improvements. The worst schooling is in the country
districts. However with the rapid social and economic change
taking place in the German countryside, the differences between
town and country are rapidly being eliminated, and this is
beginning to affect education. Whether the rural inhabitants
will be any happier is another story, but they will, in increasing
measure, have the same opportunities as in towns. The con-
fessional school is also – many would think – an unhappy
feature of the German scene, but one which receives steadily
less support from younger Catholics; in the longer run it seems
bound to dwindle. The day release/apprentice system, even if
it needs reform, does provide a comprehensive basis for industrial training, to which there is as yet no parallel in France
or the United Kingdom.

There remains the general criticism of the divided school
system. There has been considerable discussion on the 'comprehensive school' (*Gesamtschule*) and, although little has so
far been done to implement it, the concept is gaining more
adherents and the practical problems are being thoroughly
aired. There will at least be no schemes for taking several
schools miles apart and calling them a comprehensive school.
The German Federation of Trade Unions (D.G.B.) has called
for a system of *Kindergarten*, *Gesamtschule*, and *Gesamthoch-
schule*. There can be little doubt that a system on these lines
will ultimately emerge. It is, after all, the American system and
the general trends in American society have an unmistakeable
tendency to occur a few decades later in Europe.

[1] Dahrendorf, *Gesellschaft und Freiheit* (Munich, 1963), p. 285 ff. See also his
Society and Democracy in Germany (London, 1968).
[2] D. Picht. Munich: Deutscher Taschenbuch Verlag.

The Universities

The German Universities have an importance far exceeding the number studying in them. Firstly they have often nurtured new social movements – the *Burschenschaften* and other nationalistic student movements in the early nineteenth century, National Socialism in the Weimar Republic[1], the 'New Left' movement since the late 1960s. Secondly, academic research and the supply of highly qualified persons for leading posts in government, industry and science, play an important role in a modern economy. The remarkable German economic and scientific achievements of the late nineteenth century owed much to the excellence of German Universities. But West German Universities find themselves today in a profound crisis, which raises issues concerning the very future of liberal democracy in the Federal Republic. To explain the crisis in German Universities, a brief outline of their history is needed.

The Humboldtian University

German Universities are old. All the fifteen Universities which existed in the Western zones after 1945 date from the eighteenth century or earlier. The Free University of Berlin and the universities of Mainz and Saarbrücken were founded in the immediate postwar period, and three others (Konstanz, Bochum and Bremen) in the 1960s. The distinctive character of the German University, as it existed until very recently, was formed in 1809, when the University of Berlin was founded by the Prussian scholar and administrator Wilhelm von Humboldt (1767-1835). His ideas influenced not only other German Universities, but also the Universities founded in Britain in the nineteenth century. German Universities in the eighteenth century had been largely controlled by the church or local princes. Humboldt introduced 'academic freedom'. This meant that the qualified teachers – the Professors – were free to pursue research and publish the results, without political or dogmatic interference. They were in fact expected to pursue research as well as teaching students

---

[1] It is not generally realised how much student movements contributed, directly or indirectly, to the growth of National Socialism: see Hans Peter Bleuel & Ernst Klinnert, *Deutsche Studenten auf dem Weg ins Dritte Reich, Ideologien, Programme, Aktionen 1918–1935* (Gütersloh: Mohn, 1967).

(*Einheit von Forschung und Lehre*). 'Academic freedom' also meant that students were not treated like schoolchildren, with constant supervision and fixed courses of study, but were free to study what and how they pleased. They were even free to move from one University to another. To obtain qualifications, they had to take an examination at the end of their studies, but otherwise they were free. Moreover the possession of the *Abitur* gave a student the *right* to enrol at any University; he did not have to apply for admission as in the United Kingdom. But how he supported himself was considered to be his affair. The Federal Republic has introduced some student grants, but fifty-five per cent of undergraduates are still supported by their parents.

The road to a professorial Chair was hard. It was first necessary to obtain a doctorate, and then to be accepted as an assistant to a Professor. The assistant, after producing a distinguished piece of research, could then apply for the *Habilitation*, or right to lecture. For this the research work had to be approved by the Faculty (i.e. the Professors) and the candidate had satisfactorily to give a public lecture. The *Habilitation* did not in itself alter the duties of the assistant, but it made him eligible to accept a 'call' (*Ruf*) to a Chair at another University, if it came. Until he succeeded in himself becoming a Professor (or *Ordinarius*) the assistant was often in an unenviable position, being poorly paid, with no security of tenure, and heavily dependent on the favour of his own Professor. Assistants who failed to obtain a Chair usually left University work. The University was administered by the Professors in council (*Senat*), and one of them was annually elected to be chief officer (*Rektor*) on a part-time basis. Each Professor gave lectures in his field, but there was little in the way of an organised system of courses, or a formalised examination system. Professors tended to lecture on subjects that interested them, and examined students orally.

The principles enunciated by Humboldt were in many ways highly beneficial. The freeing of the Universities from political and religious control, and the introduction of high intellectual qualifications for Professors, led to the German academic eminence in the nineteenth century, which in many fields – such as chemistry – contributed to Germany's rapid economic growth in the latter part of the century. The Universities however refused to accept the more applied forms of science. The result was the setting-up of advanced technical colleges (*Technische Hochschulen*) which contributed even more directly to the German economy. In the *Technische Hochschulen* (recently renamed *Technische Universitäten*) there was a more organised system of tuition and examination, more on the lines of British and American Universities.

The National Socialist regime meant the end of academic freedom in German Universities. The government appointed a politically reliable Rector, who laid down the ideological line for the staff. The effect was disastrous. Many of the best academics went into exile or retirement, and research in many fields was crippled.

University Reform

After the war, the Universities were recreated in basically the same form as before 1933. The first generation of students were ex-Servicemen, anxious to complete their studies in the shortest time. But as students from the schools of the Federal Republic began to enter the Universities in ever-increasing numbers, the defects of the University system became more

Table 41

NUMBER OF STUDENTS IN HIGHER EDUCATION

	Germany (F.R.) 1966/7	France 1965/6
Technology	105,762	47,566
Pure Science	40,542	139,884
Medicine	44,496	61,790
Arts	64,801	142,604
Law	24,999	77,114
Social Studies	51,475	7,728
Others	20,203	12,590
Total	352,278	489,276

Source: *Basic Statistics of the Community*.

apparent. One problem was that the staff numbers and facilities were not expanded to anything like the same extent as the growth in student numbers. This was due partly to a reluctance by the *Länder* to spend money on expanding Universities or founding new ones, but also to the organisation of the Universities. The 'one Professor per subject' arrangement made it difficult to increase the number of Professors, and the absence of full-time administrators also militated against staff expansion or effective organisation. The result was that in the popular subjects there ceased to be any personal contact of the Professors with students, or any organised guidance. New students were simply presented with a list of lectures, and spent the first term wandering from one grossly overcrowded lecture theatre to another. Only in some of the less popular subjects did a tolerable staff–student ratio enable the system to work well (for example, in the agricultural economics institute in which the author undertook research in the mid 1960s). The defects of the old '*Ordinariusuniversität*' not only affected teaching, but also made organised team research almost impossible; there was consequently a tendency for research to shift to special research institutes outside – although sometimes linked with – the Universities. In economics, the best research on current problems is now undertaken by bodies such as the *I.F.O. Institut* in Munich or the *Institut für Weltwirtschaft* in Kiel.

By the late 1950s it was clear – at least to Anglo-Saxon visitors – that the system would have to be drastically reformed. The author hoped that the German Universities would adopt the best features of the American system – the collegial relation of all teachers, with the departmental head merely first among equals; the organised system of student guidance, courses and examinations; the control of administration by a full-time Faculty Dean – without losing some of the attractive features of the traditional German system, such as students' freedom to move from one University to another. Pleas for reform were made by eminent academics such as Professors Schelsky, Dahrendorf and Löwenthal. These non-Marxist sociologists and political scientists stressed the need for a system which would both meet the needs of modern society for large numbers of highly trained personnel, while preserving the traditional autonomy of Universities in purely academic matters. This would involve raising the status of non-professional staff and increasing the total numbers of staff, introducing a more organised system of teaching, and handing over some administration to full-time administrators. Endless discussions took place on reforming the Universities, but the conservatism of many Professors, the rigidity of the system, and the unwillingness of the political authorities to intervene, thwarted any substantial reform. (The sociologist Helmut Schelsky observed, in an historical survey, that the German Universities had *never* proved capable of reforming themselves.)[1]

The situation finally exploded at the end of the 1960s, when the dissatisfaction with the specific failings of West German Universities fused with the world-wide 'protest' movement of the young. The generation which was studying at German Universities in the late 1960s was the second generation of the Cold War. They had no personal experience of the rebuilding of the German economy, of the Stalinist terror and the subjugation of Eastern Europe which led to German rearmament and the formation of NATO, of the dogmatic Communist suppression of free discussion in – ironically enough – the Humboldt University in Berlin which led staff and students to create the Free University of Berlin. To many of them there seemed little to choose between Communism and Western society, and – like many previous generations of German students – they yearned for a simple utopian faith. The result was a rapid growth of assorted revolutionary doctrines – Marxism, anarchism, Maoism – which rejected liberal values and saw hope only in the destruction of the 'capitalist' system, of which they considered the Universities to be a part. These groups received support from many students who did not necessarily share their political views, but wished to change the demonstrably unsatisfactory state of affairs in the Universities. The outcome was a series of riots and student disturbances in 1967/8 which started with demonstrations in Berlin against the Shah of Persia but continued with strikes, disruption of lectures and Senate meetings, and assaults on Professors at Universities throughout the Federal Republic. These disturbances alarmed the politicians, who had till then ignored the Universities. But instead of tackling the well-known *academic* failings of the Universities, the politicians (and journalists) accepted uncritically the political-based analysis and proposals put forward by the radical groups who spearheaded the violence.

[1] *Einsamkeit und Freiheit* (Rowohlt, 1963), 2nd ed. 1971.

The argument they put forward was as follows: the trouble with the Universities was that they were not 'democratic'. In a democratic society, all institutions should be democratic, but the Universities were run by an oligarchy of Professors who used their position to further their own ends. The solution was 'democratic control' of the Universities by bodies representing the three interests involved – the students, the assistants and the professors – each with equal voting strength (*Drittelparität*). These democratic elected bodies would control all aspects of University administration, including professorial appointments. Being democratic, they would correct the politically conservative bias in previous University appointments, and would maintain a balance between 'progressive' and 'bourgeois' appointments. This argument is open to serious objections of principle discussed below. Moreover, it was often put forward by militants whose explicit aim was not any kind of 'balance' but the elimination of alternative views and gaining control of Universities as a means of gradually extending control over all the organs of society. However the demand for 'democratic' control, accompanied by all-too-justified criticisms of professional rule, seemed superficially plausible, and was widely accepted by the political parties, especially the Social Democrats. A series of *Länder* laws were passed, laying down that Universities are to be run by bodies elected on '*Drittelparität*' lines, and arrangements of this type have been introduced in most Universities.

The results so far have been disastrous. The traditional system of a University government has been destroyed, without introducing a new one. Professors and student representatives spend hours in interminable meetings, but virtually no progress has been achieved to making the Universities better places for teaching and research. Moreover violent demonstrations and harassment of individual professors has continued, causing frequent premature retirements or deaths. (The latter, ironically, included Professor Theodor Adorno of Frankfurt, one of the intellectual fathers of the New Left. The Professor fell foul of a group of students and was unable to cope with incidents like girls undressing in lectures and making improper advances.) The main effect of the changes had been to greatly increase the influence of radical-Left students, who are often the most vigorous in seeking election, and this has had a marked influence on the political colouring of professional appointments and the character of many University institutes. The appointments in social science in the New University of Bremen have been almost exclusively Marxist, while many institutes in the Free University of Berlin have ceased to be centres of learning and discussion, and become more organisations for the dogmatic propagation of revolutionary doctrines.

The Bund Freiheit der Wissenschaft

Are these developments merely teething troubles, or do they reflect a basic error in the whole 'democratising' approach? In a short book,[1] Professor Löwenthal argues eloquently and convincingly that the approach adopted is fundamentally misguided, and puts forward principles for reform. His views represent those of a group of academics, *Bund Freiheit der Wissenschaft*, founded in 1970. Professor Löwenthal poses the basic question: what is the function of a University in present-day society? He concludes that it has three functions, each requiring a different relation to society. One is the training of large numbers of qualified personnel for various occupations. In this field the University cannot be fully autonomous; it must collaborate with government and professions on the basic nature of the training. Secondly the University has the responsibility of furthering research and training academics, and in this field the qualified academics of the University must be given complete autonomy. A third function is political, in the broad sense of training students to be responsible and critical members of a pluralistic democracy. This requires both a recognition of responsibility to society, but also the ability to take a detached and critical view of society; given these conditions, the University can be left free in the carrying out of this function.

Both the Humboldtian University and the 'democratic' University set up under the new laws have failed to fulfil these functions. The Humboldtian University was designed to train only a small social *élite*, and was incapable of meeting the need for giving advanced training to a large proportion of the population. But the militants who largely control the 'demo-

[1] *Hochschule für die Demokratie: Grundlinien für eine sinnvolle Hochschulreform* (Köln: Markus-Verlag, 1971).

cratic' Universities reject the whole concept of training students for the needs of 'capitalist' society – and have ensured that the new University laws do not concede any say in the syllabus to professional or public bodies. They demand that society, while financing the Universities, should renounce any influence on the scope of undergraduate training. This is a kind of autonomy which modern society could not concede even to the traditional University, and still less to a University hostile to the whole basis of existing society.

There is, admittedly, a more fundamental question, whether society is justified in demanding trained personnel, whether there is a need for what is conveniently summed up in the term *Leistungsgesellschaft*, i.e. a society in which achievement is fostered and persons of outstanding achievement given the most responsible posts. Many of the student radicals argue that economic growth is unnecessary and even undesirable; all that is needed is to redistribute existing wealth. Therefore Universities should concern themselves with values rather than intellectual achievements – which is one argument for abolishing formal training and examinations. Professor Löwenthal rejects this argument. The Western countries have, admittedly, reached a relatively high level of affluence but face serious problems of pollution, of the control of weapons of mass destruction, of social organisation, as well as of helping the less developed countries. These are all complex intellectual problems, in which good intentions are not enough. Therefore the development and testing of applied intellectual ability is still essential.

The second function of a University is the advancement of knowledge and the training of future academics. In this field, the principle of 'academic freedom' embodied in the Humboldtian University remains as valid as ever. The only way of advancing knowledge is, on past experience, to give complete freedom to qualified academics to investigate and discuss, in an atmosphere where only facts and logic are accepted as arguments. Political interference in this field leads to intellectual and practical disasters such as 'German physics' under the National Socialists or 'communist plant breeding' under Stalin. The 'politicised' Universities system has failed in this function. There is no reasoned pursuit of truth. Since 'non-progressive' views have been eliminated, research becomes simply a matter of showing how the accepted doctrine can be applied, and teaching mere propaganda.

The attempt at *Gleichschaltung* at several Universities under the new system of University government arises from giving a dominant role in academic policy to students (undergraduates and the doctoral students who make up part of the *Assistenten*). Students are, by definition, unqualified, and hence unfitted to decide on academic questions such as the nature of research, the basic objectives of instruction and staff appointments (although teachers should welcome comments on teaching methods and be prepared to discuss, and give serious considera-tion to student views on the fundamental assumptions of their discipline). Students are inclined to simple dogmatic beliefs and intellectual fashions. That they should challenge their teachers is healthy. But when they – through elected representatives – are put in charge of academic institutes, the effect is to encourage the intolerant assertion of a currently fashionable doctrine, and to drive out the detached, rational analysis which is the Universities' main contribution to civilisation.

The third function of a University lies in the training of students to be citizens of a pluralistic democracy. This is a field in which German institutions – including Universities – have in the past been defective. One of the Prussian characteristics which were incorporated in the Bismarckian *Reich* was the principle of doing one's duty and obeying authority without question. In the Universities, professors tended to avoid teaching on current issues, even if they were historians or social scientists. Thus when the National Socialist agitation began, many professors took the line 'I am merely a plant breeder, linguist, etc.: I cannot concern myself with politics'. In spite of some notable exceptions (Löwenthal, Golo Mann, Dahrendorf, in the social sciences; Heisenberg, von Weizsäcker, in the physical sciences; and others) this tradition continued in the Federal Republic. There was little attempt to give students an understanding of the social, economic and political functioning of the Federal Republic, partly because the fragmented organisa-tion of the University prevented any organised *Grundstudium*. Even in subjects such as economics, the attempt (not confined to West Germany) to keep analysis 'value free' often made the tuition seem remote from real problems, and created the impression that the totalitarians were the only people who cared deeply about the state of the world. There was often force in the complaint of the student militants that they were being trained by – and trained to be – *Fachidioten*, i.e. specialists with limited horizons (even though there is, of course, no greater *Fachidiot* than the half-educated sociologist who often uses such terms). The current situation in the 'politicised' institutes is different, but equally unsatisfactory. Here there is no training in citizenship, merely in how to undermine 'bourgeois' society. It is hard to believe that West German taxpayers will indefinitely finance Universities which are openly hostile to the whole basis of the Federal Republic.

If the approach of both the *Fachidiot* and the 'politiciser' is rejected, what is needed? It is admittedly very difficult to train for citizenship in a pluralistic democracy. But what is surely needed is a training in rational discussion, which one seeks to understand the other points of view, to convince those of differing opinions by argument in an atmosphere of good-humoured toleration, and if possible to reach agreed positions. Such an attitude can permeate all disciplines, and not merely the study of society. There is not much of this attitude in West German Universities today.

But what of the argument, implicitly accepted by the *Hochschulgesetze*, that in a democratic society, all institutions, including Universities, should be democratically run, by committees representing the various interests? This, argues Professor Löwenthal, is a crass misunderstanding of the nature of democracy and of academic institutions. In a political democracy, different people, and different groups, have differing views as to how society should be organised, and different interests. Since a democratic society accepts that one man's view is as good as another's, we seek to reconcile these views and interests through a system of representative democracy. But functional organisations have a different purpose and are organised in a different way. When a democratic government adopts a policy, and instructs the civil service to implement it, the representatives of the various civil service grades do not hold a meeting to decide whether to implement it or not – instructions are, quite rightly, passed down the line. This does not imply blind 'Captain of Köpenick' type obedience: there can be decentralisation and feed-back of information. Moreover the civil servants are free to discuss the general issues and make their views known. But basically the civil service is there to carry out policies decided by the democratic government.

To some extent – in its capacity as a training ground for skilled personnel – a modern state-financed University is in a similar position; it cannot ignore society's needs as expressed through public and professional bodies. But a University differs from both a political system and a functional organisation in that it carries out teaching and research. The distinction between teachers and taught is not that between two groups whose differing interests have to be reconciled. It is that the teachers know more than the students, and that they remain while the students change. The responsibility for teaching and research must therefore remain with the academically qualified staff. The principle of a governing body representing the divergent interests of teachers and students is fundamentally misguided. These points might seem obvious, had they not been completely overlooked by the politicians who have framed the new University constitutions.

And yet there was a kernel of truth in the 'democratising' argument which lent it plausibility. There *was* a divergence of interest under the old system between the professors and the qualified assistants (i.e. those with the *Habilitation*, or at least the doctorate) who were often doing professorial work without professorial status or salary. Moreover there was a strong public interest in raising the status of qualified assistants, as part of a change in the system which would permit a big increase in teaching staff and a better integration of courses. As the Universities themselves proved incapable of making this change, it was necessary for the state to intervene. But the change should have been a once-for-all change in the organisation of teaching staff, with clear *educational* objectives. The changes actually introduced only make sense on the assumption that there are *permanent* and *political* differences of interests between professors, assistants and students, which need to be reconciled through a democratic procedure – an untenable view based on superficial analysis.

Professor Löwenthal, and the *Bund Freiheit der Wissenschaft* therefore reject the *Drittelparität* approach which has been imposed on the German Universities as misguided and educationally pernicious. They plead for a reform which would deal with the educational failings of the Universities and produce Universities in which a larger number of qualified staff, of more equal status, could be organised so as to produce effective teaching programmes (which still do not exist in most Universities), maintain rational scholarship, and prepare students for a pluralistic democracy. They also plead for changes in the school system and University scholarship arrangements, which will enable more children from working-class families and rural areas to attend Universities. These views have been misrepresented (for example by the *Spiegel*) as an attempt by reactionary professors to maintain the old system, and have not received serious consideration by the political parties. The Social Democratic Party in particular is for the most part critical of the *Bund Freiheit der Wissenschaft*, and several local associations have proposed that any member of it should be expelled from the Party.

The present situation in West German Universities can hardly be viewed with satisfaction by any except the avowed enemies of pluralistic democracy. Many institutes of Universities and Colleges of Education have become little more than Marxist indoctrination centres. Many professors have trimmed their sails to the new wind, just as many did under the National Socialists, and those who defend liberal democracy and the mixed economy are often subject to harassment from radical students and disapproval from 'progressive' University Presidents.

Those most concerned with them take differing views of the future of German Universities. Professor Schelsky, in a deeply pessimistic book, foresees their end as institutions of higher learning and research.[1] Other Professors see the present troubles as a passing phase, from which the Universities will emerge far better than before. But whether one is optimistic or pessimistic, there is no doubt that the old German University is dead, while the new one is not yet in sight.

Epilogue

I have devoted considerable space to the Universities because their present state, and the policies towards them adopted by

[1] *Abscheid von der Hochschulreform* (Bielefeld: Bertelsmann, 1969)

the political authorities, seems to me to be by far the most disturbing aspect of the Federal Republic (which on the whole I assess favourably). What is so disturbing is not that old institutions have been overtaken by events; that is a common predicament. Nor that they are a battlefield for the 'protest' movement of the youth; that is a world-wide phenomenon even if its German manifestation is characteristically 'thorough' and ruthless. What is so disturbing is that the political authorities, completely misunderstanding the nature of the problem, have accepted 'solutions' which have the effect of turning the Universities into bastions of totalitarian movements profoundly hostile to the Federal Republic. The leaders of the Federal Republic seem to be positively encouraging the undermining of the state. The future, for both intellectual honesty and pluralistic democracy, will be gloomy in the Federal Republic unless its leaders show more confidence in their form of society and a better understanding of its enemies than they have so far shown over the reform of the Universities.

9 Housing

The Federal Republic's most distinctive achievement is probably in the field of housing and town and country planning. The quantity of building is a great accomplishment, but an even greater one is its quality. Admittedly mistakes were made in the early days, when the need to provide homes was so pressing, and some German planners and architects are very critical of what has been achieved, although hard pressed to name any country that has done better.

It is true that the growth of car ownership and its consequences was underestimated, but traffic planning is now being tackled far more vigorously than in Britain or France, not only by building roads and providing pedestrian precincts, but also by maintaining and extending a public transport system based on modern single-decker trams (often going underground in city centres), buses and underground railways. West Germany has to some extent suffered from the tower block fad and suburban sprawl with inadequate transport facilities but most new housing is attractive and for an Englishman the most striking impression left by the rebuilt German towns is how well they have been planned and built. Some unexpected people have been impressed with the evidence of their own eyes. In a letter to *The Times* (1 January 1966) Mr Frank Allaun, M.P., wrote 'The people of most British industrial towns would go green with envy if they could see the massive housing projects being completed in the Federal Republic.' Coming from one of the most vocal advocates of housing policies diametrically opposed to those adopted in West Germany, this is impressive testimony.

Part of the explanation lies no doubt in national character and architectural tradition. This is not the first time that Germany has turned to reconstruction after a devastating war, and achieved results of great distinction. After the Thirty Years War in the seventeenth century there was the flowering of baroque architecture. Moreover the reaction against the excesses of early nineteenth century town development – which were in any case less than in Great Britain as a result of the later Industrial Revolution – began earlier. Some excellent ventures in town and country planning were carried out by German municipalities from the turn of the century onwards. Thus town planning and architecture had, by 1933, acquired a tradition and a self-confidence that they did not possess in Great Britain. After the Nazi interlude of pompous vulgarity, and the destruction of the War, it was this tradition that was again taken up in the Federal Republic. But a good deal of the explanation lies in the policies for housing (and local government and town planning) that have been adopted. Housing policy is, perhaps, the clearest example of the 'social market economy'.

The Postwar Situation

The housing situation in postwar Germany was catastrophic. As a result of war damage, over a fifth of the prewar housing stock had been either completely destroyed or rendered uninhabitable. In the larger towns, the proportion was much higher – generally over one half. At the same time the population was increased by the inflow of, in all, 13 million refugees and expellees from the East. Thus in the early postwar years there was gross overcrowding, and many families lived in wooden huts and other makeshift accommodation.

With the founding of the Federal Republic in 1949, the housing programme quickly got into its swing. By 1951 the

Table 42

POPULATION AND HOUSING STOCK
FEDERAL REPUBLIC (INCLUDING BERLIN)

	Population	Number of dwellings
	(million)	
1939	43·0	11·8
1945	about 46·0	9·4
1950	50·8	10·3
1956	53·2	10·8
1961	56·2	16·4
1970	60·7	20·8
1971	61·5	21·3

Source: *Statistisches Jahrbuch*

number of completions exceeded 400,000 a year. By 1953 it exceeded 500,000 and it has since generally ranged between 500,000 and 600,000. Between 1949 and the end of 1971 over 12 million dwellings were built, of which roughly 8 millions were for renting and 4 million for owner-occupation.

Table 43

DWELLINGS COMPLETED IN WEST GERMANY (INCLUDING WEST BERLIN)

	Total	Publicly assisted social housing	One- or two-family houses	Average floor area	% with central heating
	000			sq. ft.	%
1949	222	153	54		
1952	461	318	108	590	
1953	540	310	123	598	6
1954	572	302	139	623	7
1960	574	263	169	758	31
1966	605	204	198	867	76
1967	572	193	185	880	83
1968	520	178	165	888	88
1969	500	183	159	889	91
1970	478	137	154	903	94
1971	553	149	178	904	96

Source: *Bundesbaublatt.*

The Background

Housing policy in West Germany needs to be seen in historical perspective. With the great increase in urban population in the nineteenth century, the typical form of housing in the larger German towns became blocks of rented flats, owned by private landlords. Although these flats were not slums, they were often cramped and gloomy, as the popular name *Mietkasernen* (rent barracks) implied. After the 1914–18 War, under the influence of 'Garden City' ideas, considerable public attention was devoted to providing better housing for the mass of people, and many non-profit-making housing associations were formed, either on a co-operative basis or under the auspices of church or trade and professional bodies. The associations mostly provided flats to let, although there were some semi-rural settlements.

The terrace house characteristic of Britain in the nineteenth century, and the semi-detached house of the inter-war period, was virtually unknown, and it was usual for people of all classes to rent rather than own. Indeed it still is, although owner-occupiership is now increasing among new dwellings.

In the 1920s, many towns began local authority housing, but this was generally found to be unsatisfactory. The tenants did not look after the dwellings very well, and it was found that there were political objections to the local authority being actively engaged in providing housing for certain sections of the community. Attention was therefore switched to giving support to housing associations; these survived the Nazi period, which was characterised by rent control and neglect of housing, and under the Federal Republic they have expanded their activities considerably.

Another group of organisations set up in the 1920s, which have played a most important role in post-1945 policy, were the *Heimstätten* (home centres). Unlike the housing associations, which were private organisations, the *Heimstätten* were 'organs of public housing policy'. Their legal status is a type of non-profit-making company in which the state is joint share-holder with other bodies. The *Heimstätten* were originally set up on a provincial basis, and are now organised within the eleven *Länder*. The provincial government is the largest shareholder, others being local authorities, housing associations, banks, insurance companies etc. The *Heimstätten* do not normally build houses themselves; their function is to provide architectural, legal and financial services to housing associations, firms or individuals wishing to build. They have with the years built up architectural departments of high quality, and have been able to exercise a considerable, and very salutary influence on domestic architecture.

Postwar Policy

The housing policy of the Federal Republic can best be considered under the headings of rent control: the programme for new housing, including subsidies; and the organisation of what might be termed the house-providing industry (which is wider than the building industry in the narrow sense). All these aspects show a blend of 'social' and 'economic' considerations, which has varied according to conditions in different postwar periods.

The housing shortage was so severe at the end of the war that freeing rents would have caused them to soar. Rent control was therefore retained for nearly all existing dwellings, at first at the levels frozen since the 1930s. The controlled rents were subsequently raised from time to time. The tenants of these pre-1948 rent-controlled dwellings also enjoyed complete security of tenure. It was generally felt however that rent control was an anomalous element of 'control economy' in the 'social market economy'; it penalised owners unfairly, discouraged maintenance, and ought, it was felt, to be ended as soon as the improvement in the housing situation made this possible. Thus in 1960 an Act was passed 'for the dismantling of the control economy and for a social tenancy law'. This Act began a process of gradually ending the rent control of pre-1948 dwellings, carried out district by district according to the prevailing shortage. In each district (*Kreis*) the hypothetical housing shortage was calculated by means of a formula relating the number of households to the number of dwellings. (This information is available because everyone has to register their place of residence with the local authority.) When the housing shortage, as measured in this way, fell below 3 %, rent control was lifted. From 1965 onward, rent control was gradually lifted, and a free market established in rented housing. The remaining exceptions are Berlin, Hamburg and Munich.

In spite of some complaints, decontrol has on the whole proceeded smoothly. There was however strong pressure from the tenants' associations for giving tenants greater protection against eviction than that provided for in the decontrol Act. This Act was not unmindful of tenants' interests; a 'social clause' provided that a landlord had to give a period of notice ranging from three months to a year according to the length of occupation, and there was also a right of appeal to the courts, who could grant a stay of eviction in cases of hardship. The courts however interpreted this in a very narrow sense. As a result of an initiative from the Social Democrats, the 'Grand Coalition' Government introduced a new 'social clause' in 1967, which supplements the previous one. These provisions, although representing primarily the thinking of the Social Democrats, are quite different in approach from the legislation on rents passed by British Labour governments, which is based on the idea that the provision of rented housing is not an appropriate activity for private enterprise.

The 1967 'social clause' was justified as a means of establishing a 'partnership relationship' between landlord and tenant, giving the tenant special protection because of the importance of housing in family life, but also taking into account any legitimate interest that the landlord may have in ending the tenancy. The landlord is obliged to give a tenant his reasons for wishing to end a lease, and the tenant to give his reasons for wishing to oppose its ending. If they cannot come to some agreement, the tenant can appeal to the courts for a stay of eviction, and the courts have the power to order a continuation of the lease, at the existing rent. The criterion for continuing the lease is that its termination would cause hardship to the tenant and his family, which could not be justified, taking into account the legitimate interests of the landlord. In 1971 the Brandt Government strengthened the 'social clause' by, for example, laying down that the availability of other housing has to be taken into account. There are also laws which forbid the charging of 'extortionate' rents – a vague criterion, interpreted by reference to the prevailing rent level in the locality. The present laws provide a considerable degree of protection against sudden or arbitrary eviction, without undermining the principle of a free housing market.

Since 1967 however a very different view has gained increasing support, especially in the S.P.D. This is the view of those who do not desire the socially responsible market economy which has so far been the basis of housing policy in the Federal Republic, but wish to supplant private ownership and the market economy by a system of comprehensive state ownership and control. The 'Young Socialists' are quite clear in their aims – the nationalisation of land and the elimination of private house ownership. Much of the S.P.D. leadership, while viewing the 'Young Socialist' approach with reserve, has begun to adopt a 'pragmatic' approach which lacks any clear philosophy. The Brandt Cabinet at one stage seriously considered introducing rent control, and was only persuaded by Professor Schiller that such a step would not be *'systemkonform'*. The D.G.B., similarly, has come out with a somewhat confused collection of proposals, including a vehemently advocated but unclear 'land reform' and more security for tenants.

Housing Allowances

The decontrol of pre-1948 dwellings means that tenants of these dwellings have to pay increased rents. To alleviate hardship, the process of decontrol has been accompanied by the introduction of personal housing allowances for which all persons and any type of housing are eligible.

These housing allowances were introduced on a limited extent in the 1956 Housing Act, but under subsequent Acts – especially the second *Wohngeldgesetz* of 1970 – they were extended to all housing, and made a permanent part of official housing policy, 'in order to avoid social hardship, to make financially possible for an occupant a basic minimum of living space'. The Acts provide a right to a rent subsidy which will enable the family to pay for a basic minimum of housing. The details are however complicated (and the administration expensive). Broadly speaking, a maximum floor area is laid down for various sizes of family. A 'tolerable rent' is then calculated on the basis of family income and family circumstances expressed as a percentage – ranging from 5 to 22% of net family income. The family can then claim the difference between the 'tolerable rent' and the actual rent of a dwelling of the prescribed size, provided the rent per square metre does not exceed a certain figure. The principle of a personal housing subsidy for families in need is now an established part of the housing policy of the Federal Republic, and expenditure has risen to around D.M. 600 million a year.

The Programme for New Housing

Although the decontrol of the pre-1948 houses is complete, there is still a large proportion of dwellings whose rents are regulated, and whose tenants enjoy virtual security of tenure; the 5·5 million 'social' dwellings built since 1949, and dwellings other than 'social' ones, let by housing associations. These two types need to be explained.

The Housing Act of 1950 introduced a comprehensive system of financial assistance or taxation privileges for various types of housing. Thus dwellings built since 1950 fall into main categories:

(1) privately financed dwellings (of which some enjoy tax concessions).

(2) dwellings provided under the publicly-assisted social housing programme.

For rented dwellings a further distinction in that between:

(1) dwellings provided by housing associations.

(2) dwellings provided by firms or individuals.

The housing associations are freed from taxation in return for certain obligations. They have in recent years operated mainly under the publicly-assisted social housing programme, but this is not inevitable; they could operate independently, and are increasingly doing so.

Privately-financed Housing

The privately-financed dwellings are those built for letting or for owner-occupation which do not receive any special assistance. They do however qualify for certain general grants and tax allowances. For example, individuals who enter into a contract to save regularly towards the cost of building a house obtain at the end a premium of up to 35% from the state. And flats built to let receive a depreciation allowance, which at present falls from 3·5% to 1% per year over a 50-year period. A depreciation allowance of this type, which is granted in all countries for machinery, is a normal counterpart to Income Tax,

Table 44

SPONSORS (BAUHERREN) OF NEW HOUSING 1967

	All Housing		Social Housing
Private individuals*	58·4	Housing associations	52·2
Housing associations	19·8	Private individuals*	32·2
Building firms	12·0	Building firms	8·0
Other firms	7·8	Other firms	5·0
Public authorities	2·0	Public authorities	2·6
	100·0		100·0

Source: *Bundesbaublatt*.

* Includes houses and flats bought through housing associations.

but in the early years of the Federal Republic it was set at particular favourable rates in order to encourage the building of dwellings to let.

The belief was widely held in the early 1950s that private individuals and firms would never again be prepared to build dwellings to let, and that reliance would have to be placed on the housing associations. The housing associations have, in the event, been expanded and have made a notable contribution to the housing programme, but there has also been enormous private investment in rented housing. (German towns are full of small blocks of smart, modern flats available to let, both furnished and unfurnished, and equipped with showers and central heating; the rents, although not cheap, are tolerable in relation to incomes. To come back to English towns after living in West Germany is to experience a real shock.)

The private investment in rented housing has come partly from individuals, often builders or architects, who put up a single block, supplementing their own equity with the mortgage-type loans that are available from the lending institutions. These personal investor/entrepreneurs, who generally live on the premises, have played an important role in the providing of middle-class housing. However their personal investment is dwarfed by the institutional investment from pension and similar funds, the insurance companies claim to have invested nearly £2000 m. in rented housing since 1948. This type of investment is regarded as safe and profitable by the companies, and government policy has always welcomed it.

Owner-occupied houses and flats whose owners do not qualify for special low-interest loans also fall into the 'privately-financed' category. Houses, as distinct from flats, are generally owner-occupied, although it is very common to build either a 'two-family house' (a large detached house with a separate flat in the upper storeys) or, in the case of the popular terrace houses, to arrange rooms on the second storey floor under the roof so that they can either be let as a separate flat or used as part of the dwelling if the family is big. The house with this *Einliegerwohnung* offers a flexibility for accommodating changes in family size not found to the same extent in any other layout. The letting of a flat in a house is encouraged by provisions for setting off expenses against tax.

Housing Associations

The second group of dwellings are those leased by the housing associations. These associations date back to the 1920s, but they have received special encouragement from the Federal Republic and have expanded enormously. They are on the one hand the local co-operative housing associations, and on the other hand, those formed by various bodies such as civil servants' associations, trade unions (who finance the largest building organisation in the country, *Neue Heimat*) and the churches. The housing associations are freed from all taxation, but in return are obliged to operate on a strict non-profit-making basis. In addition to this limitation of rents to the 'cost covering' level, the associations are debarred from evicting tenants except for non-payment of rent or breaches of contract. One-third of all dwellings built since 1949, and half of all rented dwellings, have been built for letting by the housing associations, most of them under the publicly-assisted social housing programme.

Publicly-assisted Social Housing

The social housing programme was introduced in the Housing Act of 1950. Its aim was to provide dwellings for families with low incomes at subsidised rates, and a programme was laid down for building 1·8 million such dwellings between 1950 and 1956. In the event, this target was exceeded. The methods adopted for the social housing programme differed radically from those of the British local authority housing programme. Whereas in Britain subsidies were made available only to local authorities, in Germany they were made available to anyone who fulfilled the necessary qualifications and undertook the obligations which went with them. The principle was that the state provided an interest-free loan for each dwelling, which covered a large proportion, although not all of the cost, together with an annual payment in some cases. The loan could be to an individual who wished to have a house built for his own use, but, especially in the early days, it was more usually for the building of houses to let. Any individual or organisation wishing to build could obtain a loan of this type, provided that the dwellings were of certain specifications, and were let at prescribed rents to tenants who qualified for social housing by reason of their income and family circumstances. The rent is a 'cost covering' rent calculated for each dwelling according to the amount of the loan and a fixed rate of interest on the remaining capital.

In the social housing programme, the housing associations have played an important role, and have supplied roughly half the dwellings built under it. But a high proportion – in 1967 32·7% – have however been built by private individuals. This has often meant that an individual has organised the building of a small block of flats or a 'two-family house' in which he lives himself.

The tenants of dwellings built under the social housing programme enjoy security of tenure, and the rents remain at the 'cost covering' level. If however the owner of the dwelling repays the loan, the dwelling becomes decontrolled. The theory is that the money can then become available for more social housing, while the community has the advantage of the now privately-financed dwellings. The housing associations would not normally wish to take advantage of this provision, but some private owners have done so. It means of course that the tenants then either have to pay substantially higher rents – which they may or may not be willing or in a position to do – or move to housing which remains 'social'.

Another case which has attracted attention is that of tenants who obtained 'social' dwellings at low rents when they were penniless refugees, but who with the 'economic miracle' have become well off, and whose need is really less than those of young couples who do not have 'social' dwellings and have to pay higher rents. Some attempts were made to bring about a change in the law, which would enable the subsidised rents to be raised to take account of subsequent changes in tenants' incomes, but the idea met with so much opposition on legal grounds that it had to be abandoned. It is partly for this reason that, although the programme of social housing is being continued, increasing emphasis is being placed on (personal) housing allowances, which are reviewed every year, and can therefore more readily be adapted to changes in the tenants' circumstances.

With the gradual easing of the housing shortage, and the switch to indirect methods of assistance, the share of the social housing programme in total construction has declined; it went down from 56·4% of all new housing in 1953 to 36·8% in 1971. This fall partly reflects the increased emphasis on owner-occupation which was introduced by the second Housing Law of 1956. More flats are being built for owner-occupation, and increasing numbers of terrace houses have been built for owner-occupation in recent years. Although financed by individuals – with the help of various state loans or savings premiums – these houses are often built by housing associations, employing local building firms, and often using the advisory services of the *Heimstätten*. Over one-third of dwellings built since 1949 are owner-occupied. Owner-occupation has become more popular because of fears of inflation, and because more families have capital available for investment. But in West Germany – as distinct from Britain – it is not necessary to buy in order to get a place to live: there are still large numbers of flats available to rent.

The German social housing programme, in so far as it is concerned with rented housing, thus differs fundamentally from the British equivalent. In Germany, local authorities have built only an insignificant proportion of the 'social' dwellings; most of them have been built by housing associations or by individuals. As compared with the British, the German system has both administrative and social advantages. Whereas in Britain the whole burden of administration falls on local authorities, the German system enlists the energies of large numbers of people – the officials of housing associations, both full-time and part-time, as well as numerous individuals or firms with a personal or financial interest in the property.

But the social advantages of the German system are perhaps even more important. The German system has avoided the polarisation of society between council estate dwellers and owner-occupiers which many feel is producing 'two nations' in Great Britain. Although there are 'better' and 'poorer' districts, there are in Germany no council estates and few private housing estates, with all that these terms imply, both visually and socially in Great Britain. Housing which has received assistance under the social housing programme is mixed in with other housing, and is visually indistinguishable. One therefore finds a wider range of social classes living in fairly close proximity in new housing areas than is generally the case in this country. This happy result is not however merely the result of the methods adopted in the social housing programme. It is also associated with a lower degree of class-consciousness in Germany than in Britain, and with the work of the *Heimstätten*.

The *Heimstätten* must be given part of the credit for the

Table 45

RENTS (ALL DWELLINGS)

	(1962 = 100)
1965	117·7
1967	135·6
1969	156·5
1970	163·3
1971	173·0
1972	182·1

widespread adoption of building styles and methods which are both economically sound and aesthetically pleasing. The actual building is mainly carried on by private, generally small firms; there are some 67,000 firms in the building industry, occupying 1·7 million persons. However the *Heimstätten* carry out experiments with various types of construction, accumulate

Table 46

AVERAGE PRICES OF BUILDING LAND

	Land ready for building	Bare land
	D.M. per m²	D.M. per m²
1962	14·8	9·5
1966	23·6	14·6
1968	28·4	15·9
1971	33·9	19·7

Source: *Statistisches Jahrbuch.*

experience with various types of housing layout and design, and then pass on their results to firms and housing associations. The *Heimstätten* have also succeeded in bringing about a great deal of standardisation in the sizes of components. Particularly interesting and important work has been done by the *Heimstätten* in sponsoring 'demonstration housing projects' in a large number of towns, so as to popularise new housing forms. In recent years the emphasis has been on space-saving types of housing which nevertheless provide each dwelling with an 'open air room'. One type is the single-storey flat-topped 'atrium house', which can be arranged along pedestrian paths, or on the edge of parks, etc. A different approach has been to step back multi-storey buildings so as to provide a roof garden on top of the dwelling below. This can be done very successfully on steep slopes. Alternatively, low-rise blocks of flats can be stepped back so as to give the same effect, with cars housed in the central ground floor area.

Recent Developments

Although the severe housing shortage of the postwar era no longer exists, there is a continuing demand for new housing as a result of rising incomes and rising numbers of families. A comprehensive and detailed housing census was carried out in 1968.[1] This showed a total of 19·6 million dwellings: of these 61·1% were tenanted, 34·3% owner-occupied and 4·6% sub-tenanted. In spite of the increase in the quantity and quality of dwellings, there were still many pre-1939 houses which did not provide satisfactory living conditions. A million dwellings were classified as unfit for habitation and in need of replacement. As many as 6·35 million dwellings lacked a bath or shower. It was estimated that 300,000 new dwellings a year were needed to cater for the rise in population and the tendency to smaller families.

Thus the number of dwellings built each year has continued at only slightly lower a level than in the early 1960s. This has been accompanied by a rise in house prices and rents which is nearly double the general rise in prices because of rises in building costs and land prices (tables 45, 46). The average expenditure on rent in a four-person wage-earner family has risen from 10·2 to 15·5% of total expenditure. But at the same time the average floor space per family and the quality of housing has risen steadily.

[1] *Jahresbericht der Bundesregierung* (1970), p. 633.

The outlook is for a continued supply of between 400,000 and 500,000 new dwellings per year, with the emphasis being switched from mere numbers to the renovation of old buildings and the rebuilding of old housing areas. The problems of *Stadtsanierung* – with emphasis on the relation between re-building and social life, transport, employment and leisure activities – are now a major preoccupation of central and local government.

Summary

To sum up German housing policy, it is neither one of relying solely on private builders and landlords nor on local authority housing, but one which combines state intervention and private initiative. The design of housing areas is to a large extent influenced by non-profit-making bodies, but the business of building and administration is left to private firms and housing associations. The housing associations have made a substantial contribution but have not displaced the private landlord. Subsidies to provide low-rent accommodation are not linked to local authority housing, but are available to any new building when the necessary obligations are fulfilled. The subsidisation of particular dwellings is supplemented by personal housing allowances. The provision of houses to let has been financially encouraged, and rent control of older houses has been abandoned.

In terms of quantity and quality, the Federal Republic can lay claim to have had the most successful housing programme in the world, even though much remains to be done. This achievement has taken place under policies which have been consistently based on the philosophy of a 'social market economy'. But these policies are now under strong attack, and it remains to be seen whether they will be continued.

10 The Federal Republic – Retrospect and Prospect

(1) A SUMMARY OF THE MAIN STAGES IN THE DEVELOPMENT OF THE REPUBLIC

The Adenauer Era 1949–57

In the postwar years, Konrad Adenauer formed the Christian Democratic Union (C.D.U.), a moderate conservative party, alongside the long-established Social Democratic Party (S.P.D.) and the Free Democratic Party (F.D.P.). There is quite a close parallel with the Conservative, Labour and Liberal Parties in Britain respectively.

The first two governments of the Federal Republic were C.D.U./F.D.P. coalitions, in which Konrad Adenauer was Chancellor, and Ludwig Erhard Minister of Economic Affairs. These two governments set the course for the internal and external policy of the Republic. Internally there was the introduction of 'the social market economy'; the abandonment of rationing and allocations, together with the policies on housing and industrial relations introduced by the Housing Act of 1950 and the Works Constitution (*Betriebsverfassung*) Act of 1952. Externally there was the policy of close links with Western Europe and the United States, reflected in membership of the Organisation for European Economic Co-operation (1949), the European Coal and Steel Community (1951) and later the European Economic Community; rearmament and NATO membership (1955). During this period, these policies were strongly opposed by the S.P.D., which believed in nationalisation and controls, opposed rearmament and the Western alliances and advocated seeking a deal with Russia on a neutral reunited Germany.

The End of the Adenauer Era 1958–63

Although Adenauer remained Chancellor, his dominance declined, partly because the internal and external divisions became less clear-cut. In the 'Godesberg programme' (1959) the S.P.D. accepted a mixed economy and in a speech to the Bundestag, the Party Secretary, Herbert Wehner, announced the party's support for the international obligations entered into by the Federal Republic. From this time on, the S.P.D. became a serious contender for political power. Abroad, the beginning of a dialogue between the United States and Russia, and the beginnings of a rift between Western Europe and the United States, accentuated by the coming to power of General de Gaulle, complicated the previously simple issues of foreign policy. At home, the initial tasks of reconstruction had been accomplished, and attention began to turn to meeting more sophisticated consumer demands and coping with the problems of affluence.

The Erhard Government 1963–6

Dr Erhard, who had been so successful as Economics Minister, proved a disappointing Chancellor. His weakness in controlling public expenditure contributed to a boom, followed in 1966 by the first recession experienced by the Federal Republic. The C.D.U. began to be torn by personal and political differences. The 'Gaullists', led by Herr Strauss, stressed the need for a close alliance with France; the 'Atlanticists', led by Herr Schröder, emphasised the importance of the link with the United States.

The Grand Coalition 1966–9

The coalition of C.D.U. and S.P.D. allowed the C.D.U. a chance to recover, and provided the Social Democrats with the opportunity to enter government after a generation of Opposition. This government introduced important innovations in both domestic and foreign policy. A more sophisticated approach to economic policy was introduced with the Economic Stabilisation Act and medium-term economic planning. Abroad, the opening of diplomatic contacts with Yugoslavia and Rumania heralded the beginning of contact with Eastern Europe.

However, the elimination of parliamentary opposition contributed to the emergence of radical opposition groups, the National Democratic Party (N.P.D.) and the left-wing 'opposition outside Parliament' which came into prominence with the student riots of 1967. The N.P.D. was a transient phenomenon, but the Left-wing student movement represented a shift of attitudes among the rising generation which has continued.

The Brandt Government 1969–72

In the 1969 elections, the S.P.D. and the small Free Democratic Party gained a small majority and formed a government. Thus the Federal Republic showed that it was possible for the previous Opposition party to take over the government – a highly desirable development for its political health. The S.P.D. came to power promising a new *Ostpolitik* and 'internal reforms' in education, taxation and the social services. The government negotiated a treaty with Russia (1972) which accepted the existing frontiers in Europe and renounced the use of force. But very little was achieved on the internal reforms.

Unrest continued in the Universities, and there was a marked Left-ward shift among intellectuals and communicators. A revolutionary political group, known as the Baader-Meinhof gang, for a time organised spectacular bombing and shooting incidents. More important was a swing back among younger S.P.D. members to the type of policies held by the party before the Godesberg programme. A rift developed between Professor Schiller and his S.P.D. Cabinet colleagues over their inclination to adopt economic measures of a 'dirigiste' type, and over what he considered to be their irresponsible refusal to take action indicated by forecasts of a growing deficit in the budget. This rift culminated with his resignation in July 1972. But this did not prevent the S.P.D. and F.D.P. being returned with increased numbers in the election in November 1972, and forming a new coalition government.

(2) A PERSONAL VIEW

What assessments can one make of the development of the Federal Republic so far, and of its future prospects? To get this young nation into perspective, one needs to consider the extraordinary conditions of its birth. The decision by the Russians to administer their Occupation Zone completely independently, and to build a barbed-wire fence and minefield 500 miles long right across Germany, was a brutal amputation. Imagine South-East England, in the postwar years, being placed under Russian control, apart from an enclave in Westminster, with a fence stretching from Southampton to the Wash. Imagine further that all the major British cities had been bombed as badly as Coventry, and that some ten million Ugandan Asians were flooding into what was left of Great Britain, and one has some idea of the situation.

That the Federal Republic had, in some ten years, solved the main problems of housing and employment, was remarkable and praiseworthy. That it had absorbed the refugees without poisoning its whole political life was even more so. The Germans who were expelled from the territories incorporated into Poland were, after all, treated every bit as badly as the Palestinian Arab refugees or the Frenchmen expelled from Algeria, but they did not resort to assassination. (They were not, of course, kept stewing in camps for a generation like the Palestinians. But that is a measure of the success of the Federal Republic in solving a problem statistically greater than that of the Palestinians.) Moreover the regime imposed by the Red Army on East Germany was not a tyranny imposed on the people of some distant land, but on fathers, sisters, friends. It would not have been surprising if the Federal Republic really had become the revanchist state of Communist propaganda. It did not, even though (and this is something that foreigners are inclined to overlook) reunification – or at least the right of East Germans to choose their form of government, and to travel freely – is one of the Federal Republic's prime national interests.

The policy forced through by Adenauer was one of co-operation with the Western Allies, and the merging of the Federal Republic in a West European grouping, while holding out hope of eventual reunification. It is easy to point out the inconsistencies in this policy. As the Social Democrats argued at the time, rearmament and Western Alliances were incompatible with a neutralised, reunited Germany, which they believed should be offered to the Russians. But was this ever on the cards? The Western allies had originally planned to run Germany jointly with the Russians; it was the Russians and not the Western powers who split the country. There is some evidence that Malenkov, in his brief tenure of power, toyed with the idea of permitting a reunited Germany, an idea that might have been taken up more eagerly. But was it much to go on? Is it likely that the country which has unhesitatingly and ruthlessly used tanks to crush any moves for independence in Eastern Europe (East Berlin 1955, Hungary 1956, Czechoslovakia 1968) would have given up the lynch-pin of their East European empire? A more likely outcome of the original Social Democrat policy would have been a continued Russian control of East Germany, with a neutral and isolated West Germany providing a dangerous source of instability in Central Europe.

It is also clear – as many West German writers began to point out in the mid-1960s – that the policies adopted towards Poland and other East European states were wrong-headed. To maintain the fiction that the lands beyond the Oder and Neisse were still part of Germany was about as sensible as maintaining that Rhodesia is a British colony. And the 'Hallstein Doctrine' – which resulted in Bonn having no diplomatic relations with Eastern Europe – was the product of a narrow bureaucratic-legalistic mind.

And yet it seems even more clear with the passage of time that, basically, Adenauer was right. The general lines laid down by Adenauer – the formation of a West German state, linked militarily and economically with Western Europe and teh United States – in no way preclude the establishment of diplomatic relations with Eastern Europe. But any weakening of the Russian hold on Eastern Europe will be a matter of decades rather than years, and nothing that the West could have done after 1945 could have altered that situation. Adenauer was, in some ways, not an attractive man, but his greatness as a politician seems even clearer today.[1]

The subsequent course of West Germany's relations with her allies in NATO and the E.E.C. has not always been smooth, and especially in view of West Germany's growing self-confidence, there will be problems in the future. Moreover there is a need to reconsider many accepted doctrines in both the military and the economic field. In the economic field, the enlargement of the E.E.C. has contributed to a dangerous rift between Western Europe and the United States, and the attitude of the Brussels bureaucracy in preferring trade controls

[1] Terence Prittie, *Adenauer* (T. Stacey, 1972).

to flexible exchange rates is one that needs to be challenged. Fortunately there is a strong tradition in West Germany of favouring liberal international economic policies. But when one compares what has happened in Western Europe with what happened after the First World War it is hard to avoid the conclusion that – so far – it has been better this time.

Let us turn to internal policies. In the twenty-three years of its existence, very different pictures have been painted of the German Federal Republic by outsiders. In the early days, most Americans were impressed by the remarkable economic recovery and physical rebuilding, and praised the liberal system under which it was accomplished. In Britain, and to some extent France, the country did not on the whole have such a good press. To Lord Balogh or Professor Oulès, it was a quasi-fascist state, in which the workers' faces were ground into the dust for the benefit of a few rich men.[1] The Communists have never ceased to portray it as a country dominated by generals itching for a war to recover the lost territories in the East, and this view has evoked responses from the Right as well as the Left. When the (now virtually defunct) National Democrat Party gained a few parliamentary seats in 1966, the *Daily Express* asked whether anyone could now deny that the terms 'German' and 'Nazi' were synonymous.

But most Englishmen who spoke German and lived for any time in West Germany did not subscribe to these attacks. It seemed to them that the Federal Republic was on the whole a decent, liberal, democratic state which, in those fields most directly affecting the ordinary citizen – local government, firm, trade union – had much to teach Great Britain. They were impressed by the system of local and regional government, which brought decision-making much nearer to the man in the street; by a system of industrial relations which was a revelation after the squalid farce in Britain; by the huge investment in roads, public transport, theatres, and recreational facilities, through which West Germany had escaped the dangers of 'personal affluence and public squalor' better than any other major industrial country.

This more favourable view was reflected in the writings of some of the more percipient British journalists. As the deputy-

[1] See pp. ix, 70.

editor of the *Economist* wrote in an excellent survey: 'It is a hearteningly decent society that the West Germans have built up, in some shaming ways more decent than our own.'[1] Mr Terence Prittie – as German correspondent of the *Guardian*, one of the few remaining foreign correspondents allowed enough time in a country to get to know it – always brought out the admirable aspects of the new West German state.[2]

In the mid-1960s, the criticisms levelled at the Federal Republic in its early years were revived, both by old *émigrés* like Karl Jaspers and by young intellectuals of a Marxist persuasion.[3] Some of these attacks were of 'capitalism' in general, but others were aroused by specific political developments: the growth of the *Bundeswehr*, the emergency powers legislation introduced in 1966, the formation of the National Democratic Party. The unease about having an Army and emergency powers legislation was perhaps understandable in view of the dubious role played by some high *Reichswehr* officers in the Weimar Republic, and the use of emergency powers by the Brüning Government. But the view of the *Bundeswehr* and the emergency powers legislation as an attempt to introduce a fascist dictatorship were never very convincing. An Army which is so based on the 'civilian in uniform' concept that hairnets are issued, trade unions are allowed and any complaint against an officer can be investigated by an 'Ombudsman' (*Wehrbeauftragte*) is certainly very different from the *Reichswehr*. Moreover every country, quite rightly, has provisions for introducing emergency powers in an emergency, and the West German laws go to extreme lengths to prevent their being misused. (They have, of course, never been invoked.) At the same time, the N.P.D. has withered and collapsed.

But although the threat from the old guard of the Right has not materialised, a far more real threat has arisen from the young totalitarians of the Left. By the middle 1960s, it was clear that the new generation coming into the Universities were of a markedly different type than their fathers. There are in fact three generations in West Germany, with a greater gap between

[1] 'The German Lesson' in *The Economist*, p. iv (15 Oct 1966).
[2] *Germany divided: the Legacy of the Nazi Era* (1960). *Germany* ('Life' World Library, 1963).
[3] Karl Jaspers, *Wohin treibt die Bundesrepublik?* (1968).

them than in most countries. The oldest generation who were young in the twenties and thirties, were often at that time passionate Nazis. The middle generation, which grew up during the Nazi period, acquired a profound distaste for ideology. They had seen where the brave words of the Nazis had led, and wanted to simply rebuild their shattered country and live in peace. It is this generation which has built up the Federal Republic, starting off by struggling to get enough to eat, and working up to the point at which an ordinary man can ski at the weekends in winter and spend his summer holidays in Majorca. This generation was not greatly interested in politics – certainly not in violent politics. The student protesters are the generation which has grown up in the Federal Republic; to them the Nazis and the war are ancient history; they have no memory of the privations their parents suffered in the postwar period, or of the work that went into rebuilding West Germany out of the ruins. Like their grandparents, but unlike their parents, they are a political and ideological generation. This has its good side – it means a more honest examination of many of the internal and external German problems. But it also has great dangers: the previous generation was inoculated against war and revolution; the new one is not. The comparison with the Nazi movement is not unjustified. The early Nazi movement contained – in addition to thugs and psychopaths – many idealistic, decent young people who believed that 'the system' was effete and had to be violently overthrown. There is something rather frightening in the way in which idealistic, decent young Germans are today putting forward very similar views, with very little knowledge of what revolutions are really like, or how they almost invariably end up.[1]

[1] The following characteristic extract is taken from the report of a conference on 'Sozialistische Strategie in Spätkapitalismus – zur Chance der Linken in der S.P.D.' organised by the Berlin branch of the 'Young Socialists'.

'Die Alternative, Revolution oder Reformismus' ist nur eine scheinbare. Als Ausweg aus dem Dilemma bietet sich die Strategie der systemüberwindenden Reformen an. Bei der Verfolgung der Strategie der systemüberwindenden Reformen müssen autonome Machtpositionen errungen werden, die gleichbedeutend sind mit Breschen im kapitalistischen System. Diese Machtpositionen sind dann Ausgangspunkte für die Fortsetzung des Kampfes auf einer höheren Ebene. Natürlich ist es nicht möglich, sich von vornherein auf bestimmte Mittel des Kampfes festzulegen. Ob mit legalen oder illegalen, mit friedlichen Mitteln oder

In West Germany today, much seems the same as it was ten years ago. Coming from Britain, one is still struck by the cleanliness, tidiness and efficiency of everything, by the smart cafés and beautiful public buildings, the huge pedestrian areas in town centres, the splendid public transport system. It is an ordered and somewhat formal society, but one with considerable human warmth and gaiety. But go onto a University campus, and you are in another world. The first thing you notice is the litter; in a students' union it covers the floor, and one might almost imagine oneself in Britain. Then there are the posters – crudely written notices calling for the disruption of certain lectures, for demonstrations against American imperialism, for student control of the University. The students themselves vary like any other group of human beings. Some are fluent, reasonable and attractive; the general tendency however is for certain features of the international 'protest' movement – contempt for the past, sociologese, intolerance, humourlessness – to be exaggerated in a characteristically German fashion. The more energetic have a clear idea – in abstract terms – of an ideal society which will be created after the destruction of existing institutions. 'Bourgeois' morality is rejected – any action is justified which serves the cause. To arguments that this 'end justifies the means' philosophy has, ever since the French Revolution produced bestialities culminating in the Russian and Nazi prison camps; that civilisation depends on laboriously built-up institutions such as the rule of law, the acceptance of political and economic pluralism, they turn a deaf ear. One might have thought that the Germans, of all people, would have learnt from their history, but it was a German (Hegel) who concluded that the only thing one learns from history is that no one ever learns anything from history.

I find it far more difficult to forecast the future of the Federal Republic today than some years ago. In 1967, it was easy to see that the recession was merely a ripple on the surface of an immensely healthy economy, that the National Democrats were not a serious threat to West German democracy, that the republic would continue to develop internally and externally

---

mit Gewalt vorgegangen werden muss, ist keine Frage der persönlichen Neigung oder Veranlagung, sondern kann erst aus einer Analyse deuatitr Sion hervorgehen.'

along the lines laid down by its founders.[1] But in the last few years, revolutionary Left-wing doctrines have spread in the Universities and Colleges of Education extremely rapidly, and this is having an effect on schools, trade unions and the S.P.D. ('They want a completely different republic', as Professor Schiller remarked sadly after a recent meeting of the Young Socialists.) Whether they will achieve sufficient influence to turn West Germany into the China, Cuba or Allende's Chile which are their models is doubtful, but there are certainly stormy waters ahead. The only thing that can be said with confidence is that – if it is to survive – liberal democracy will have to defend itself more fluently, more self-confidently and more knowledgeably than it has done in recent years.

The Federal Republic has for the most part solved the problems of poverty and material shortage, and achieved a material standard of living higher than that of any other European country except Sweden. There are still some pockets of poverty – some pensioners not yet covered by the complex pension schemes, some farmers caught up in an agricultural revolution – but these are rapidly being eliminated. Nor does the Federal Republic suffer from serious problems of urban depressed areas. There is the special case of the immigrant workers – well paid but often poorly housed and socially un-assimilated – which may well be a time-bomb for the future, but the Federal Republic does not have 'ghettoes' of the type found in the United States and the United Kingdom.

It seems clear that the problems of the next few decades will be environmental and social rather than those of achieving economic growth. There are the problems of taming technology – cleaning up the air and the water, reducing noise, improving working conditions. But beyond that are the profound psycho-logical and social problems of man in an affluent, technological society. The elimination of poverty and war does not in itself make people happy. Indeed some human populations show disquietingly similar symptoms to the social and psychological breakdown observed by zoologists when rats are overcrowded, or certain types of bird deprived of the stresses of living in their natural habitat.

[1] G. Hallett, 'Britain and the Future of Germany', *Political Quarterly*
July, 1968

How will West Germany cope with the problems of the future? There are both encouraging and discouraging signs. At the government level, the quality of debate and decision-making seems almost to have declined. In the early years of the Federal Republic there were at least passionate debates on important issues of domestic and foreign policy, and decisive steps were taken. During the first Brandt Government, on the other hand, both government and opposition appear to have been engaged in shadow-boxing. The *Ostpolitik*, admirable enough in its way, will clearly not change the realities of power in Eastern Europe. Political terrorism was met by craven capitulation interspersed with ill-considered shooting. The 'internal reforms' were not seriously tackled, and long-term budgetary problems were pushed under the carpet. Nor did the opposition spell out real alternatives. The C.D.U./C.S.U. was openly split on the Eastern treaties, and attacked inflation without really indicating how it would cure it.

On the intellectual scene, the position is even bleaker. Faced with a new Sparta on the other side of the minefields, with military training from school onwards, strict censorship and government control of all aspects of life; the reaction of large numbers of academics, churchmen and media-men has been to lose no opportunity of ridiculing the Western system, praising the communist one, and justifying crime and violence. The *trahison des clercs* has made particularly rapid progress in the Universities. With their unique role of research and advanced training, Universities could make as great a contribution to modern society as they have ever made in the past. But as a result of the failings of the University authorities, and neglect by the federal and provincial governments, followed by mis-guided intervention, the West German Universities will probably not play this role for at least another generation.

The armed forces are in little better shape. A highly creditable attempt has been made to banish the old Prussian tradition of blind obedience and brutal discipline and introduce the principle of the 'civilian in uniform'. In recent years however these attempts have been undermined by the *malaise* which afflicts all conscript armies in democracies, when there is no obvious military threat. The conscripts, who resent being in uniform, are disaffected and undermine the morale of the regulars. At present the discipline and spirit of the *Bundeswehr* is so low as to put its effectiveness in question. These defects of peace-time conscript armies are not a specifically German phenomenon (the author can remember the squalid farce of British National Service in the late 1940s) but they have been aggravated by the currently widespread 'anti-war' feeling. The salvation of the British army lay in its transformation to an all-professional body. A similar solution has been suggested for the *Bundeswehr*, but governments are still inhibited from taking such an obvious step by memories of the Reichswehr 'state within a state' in the Weimar Republic.

And yet there is much that is encouraging in West Germany. Even among the intellectuals, there are writers like Günter Grass and University teachers like Professor Löwenthal who courageously defend liberal democracy. And there is such an extensive devolution of authority – in both political and economic affairs – and such a high general level of competence, that things get done, even when policy-making at a national level is not as decisive as might be wished. When one talks to industrialists, trade union officials, civil servants and local politicians, one is impressed by their intelligence and common-sense, their understanding of current problems, their thorough-ness in preparing plans and their ability to implement them in an astonishingly short time. Even the young Left-wing trade union officials who blithely explain the need for policies such as nationalising land, taxing away development value, or con-trolling rents, without the slightest knowledge of the unfortunate effects of such policies in, say, Britain and Sweden, have an intellectual ability which suggests that they would learn quickly from experience.

Although West Germany has a highly productive economy and a social system which compares favourably with that of any country in the world, although resources are being devoted to coping with the problems of affluence as effectively as any-where, the growth of inflation and the irrational aspects of the youth revolutionary movement cast shadows over the future. The stability of the Federal Republic in the 1950s and early 1960s almost seemed – in view of Germany's turbulent history – too good to be true, and it was. In the past the Germans, who have shown such extraordinary powers of reconstruction, have thereafter so often engaged in wild ventures which have destroyed everything they had built up. Perhaps the Germans, having achieved so much success in the Federal Republic with political and economic liberalism, will destroy what they have built up. I do not myself consider it likely. Economic and social affairs in the Federal Republic will be more chequered, complex, and probably more violent in the next twenty-three years than in its first twenty-three, but I believe that there is ground for a wary optimism. It would be ironic if the freedom prevailing in the Federal Republic engendered its own destruction. But history sometimes indulges in jokes of questionable taste.

Index